W9-AYO-351

WITHDRAWN

You matter

Ten Spiritual Commitments for a Richer and More Meaningful Life

RABBI MARK BOROVITZ
AND
PAUL BERGMAN

authorHOUSE®

AuthorHouse™
1663 Liberty Drive
Bloomington, IN 47403
www.authorhouse.com
Phone: 1 (800) 839-8640

© *2018 Rabbi Mark Borovitz and Paul Bergman. All rights reserved.*

No part of this book may be reproduced, stored in a retrieval system, or transmitted by any means without the written permission of the author.

Published by AuthorHouse 01/02/2018

ISBN: 978-1-5462-1623-0 (sc)
ISBN: 978-1-5462-1622-3 (hc)
ISBN: 978-1-5462-2331-3 (e)

Library of Congress Control Number: 2017919614

Print information available on the last page.

Any people depicted in stock imagery provided by Thinkstock are models, and such images are being used for illustrative purposes only. Certain stock imagery © Thinkstock.

This book is printed on acid-free paper.

Because of the dynamic nature of the Internet, any web addresses or links contained in this book may have changed since publication and may no longer be valid. The views expressed in this work are solely those of the author and do not necessarily reflect the views of the publisher, and the publisher hereby disclaims any responsibility for them.

Scripture taken from the New King James Version®. Copyright © 1982 by Thomas Nelson. Used by permission. All rights reserved.

CONTENTS

DEDICATIONS

RABBI MARK: I dedicate this book to Harriet and Heather, my parents, Jerry, *z"l*, and Millie, my brothers and sister, my nieces and nephews as well as my aunts, uncles and grandparents who all shaped me and the teachings of this book. I also dedicate this book to all of my teachers, Rabbis Ed Feinstein, Harold Shulweis, Jonathan Omer-Man, Mel Silverman, Aryeh Cohen, and a myriad of others. I dedicate this book to Rabbi Abraham Joshua Heschel who has shaped my soul, my thinking and my teaching as well as to Dr. Susannah Heschel who continues to be a source of inspiration and knowledge to and for me. I am deeply indebted to and dedicate this book to everyone with whom I have had the honor and pleasure of learning at Beit T'Shuvah-residents and staff, Board members and donors-you all have made this book and the amazing life I lead possible.

Paul: I dedicate this book to my wife Andrea; to my parents Rhoda and Bernie, who would be stunned to find out that I have written a book with a rabbi; to my grandchildren Francesca and Nicholas, whose very early years remind me often that life is filled with wondrous experiences; to all of my friends in the Beit T'Shuvah and Al-Anon communities, who have taught me that miracles can happen but when they don't we can help each other continue to put one foot in front of the other; and to the family members and friends who help me live with joy and gratitude.

ACKNOWLEDGMENTS

W E ARE GRATEFUL to the following people who read all or parts of earlier drafts of the book: Harriet Rossetto, Rabbi Ed Feinstein, Andrea Sossin-Bergman, Chuck Bergman, Eileen Sossin-Johnson, Bob Bendetson, Bonny Fetterman, Fred Kuperberg, Susan Rappaport and Julie Soter. Our special gratitude to Susan Reneau, whose care, experience and expertise is reflected throughout the book. We have learned from the wisdom of you all.

CHAPTER ONE

A DOORWAY

MY NAME IS Mark, and I am a recovering alcoholic and drug addict. My background includes felony convictions for fraud and theft, and two terms in California state prison. Sober today and for nearly thirty years, I am also the senior rabbi and spiritual leader of Beit T'Shuvah. Beit T'Shuvah, which is Hebrew for "House of Return," is a Los Angeles residential addiction treatment facility. Beit T'Shuvah's mission extends beyond helping people get sober. The principles and tools of its recovery program have helped many hundreds of addicts like me who have lost our way to regain our dignity and passion for life so that we can enjoy decent lives of purpose.

Beit T'Shuvah's recovery program is the basis of the ten spiritual commitments that are the focus of this book. The commitments can help all of us, addicts and non-addicts alike, improve the quality of our lives. As Beit T'Shuvah's founder Harriet Rossetto often points out, "We are all either in recovery or in denial." I understand Harriet to mean that addiction is but one type of spiritual malady that can diminish our enjoyment of life. Among other common spiritual maladies are low self-esteem, holding on to resentments, a need to appear to be "more than," a need to be right, a need to control others, fear of success, fear of change, obsession with career, and indifference to life. When we are willing to pursue recovery from our spiritual maladies, whether they have resulted in addiction or not, the principles and tools of the ten commitments diminish their power to control our actions.

I began to develop the commitments after two decades of chaos when my life centered on alcohol, drugs and crime. In a police car, on my way to a second prison term, I finally experienced a "moment of clarity." I became willing to change direction and live decently. I used my second prison term to study Jewish texts with a marvelous and caring prison chaplain, Rabbi

Mel Silverman. I also studied the Twelve Steps of Alcoholics Anonymous and regularly attended Jewish services and A.A. meetings. After my release on parole, I went to work at a small halfway house for Jewish ex-cons that Harriet Rossetto had recently started that she called Beit T'Shuvah. Though I was not then a rabbi, I conducted bi-weekly Friday night Sabbath services for the ex-cons and their families in the backyard.

Harriet's small halfway house has become one of the country's pre-eminent residential addiction treatment facilities. Its residents have come from many different religious traditions and from none at all. Many residents come straight from jails, prisons and the streets. Beit T'Shuvah never turns anyone away for lack of money. And like so many other residents and alumni of Beit T'Shuvah, I have a wondrous life that I never could have imagined and for which I am so grateful every single day.

Beit T'Shuvah is a synagogue as well as a residential treatment facility. During Friday night Sabbath services, the clergy and the congregation together welcome in new residents with a prayer that in part expresses the hope that "this house may be, for all who enter, the doorway to a richer and more meaningful life." With this same spirit, I welcome you to the ten commitments with a prayer that they will help you open your doorway to a richer and more meaningful life.

THE TEN COMMITMENTS

The ten commitments embody my understanding of the spiritual principles and traditions of Judaism and Alcoholics Anonymous. The commitments re-state the moral commands of the Bible's Ten Commandments as spiritual promises to our souls. The commitments are a pathway not to religious practice or belief but to *spiritual buoyancy*. Spiritual buoyancy results from a sense of wholeness of heart and mind that helps us experience many moments of what my hero Rabbi Abraham Joshua Heschel called "radical amazement of life." At the core of every human being is the need for connection to others and the desire for a meaningful life. The principles and tools of the commitments convert the Ten Commandments' prohibitions into life-nurturing and meaningful actions that constitute our unique answers to:

The inward-facing question, "What am I getting out of life?" and
The outward-facing question, "What is life getting out of me?"

Here in summary form are the ten commitments:

First Commitment: *I will understand God in a way that helps me to act righteously.* The daily presence of the higher power of my personal understanding reminds me that more than my personal satisfaction is at stake in all of my actions.

Second Commitment: *I will diminish resentments by practicing forgiveness.* Practicing forgiveness promotes my own well-being and builds bridges between me and other people.

Third Commitment: *I will pursue righteous actions by wrestling with my conflicting desires to act selfishly and selflessly.* I carry my understanding of my higher power into daily life by doing my best to act in a way that balances my needs and desires with those of other people.

Fourth Commitment: *I will use spiritual inventories regularly to assess my actions.* Reflecting on my actions helps me build on what I have done well and diminish my mistakes going forward.

Fifth Commitment: *I will honor my parents by acting from principle in all of my affairs.* I seek to act righteously in all circumstances, whether my actions affect friends or strangers, the powerful or the powerless.

Sixth Commitment: *I will not murder my soul; I will live by acting with daily purpose.* I will keep my spirit alive by valuing my unique talents and interests and acting on purpose.

Seventh Commitment: *I will not adulterate my soul; I will observe boundaries instead of trying to control the actions of others.* When I keep the focus on my actions, I give others the opportunity to change and grow by experiencing the consequences of their own actions.

Eighth Commitment: *I will not steal from my own soul; I will augment its strength by nurturing spiritual partnerships.* I will expand the influence of my impulse to act righteously by helping and seeking help from spiritual partners.

Ninth Commitment: *I will not lie to my own soul; I will tell myself the truth about my mistakes and misdeeds.* I will acknowledge when I have missed the mark so that I can help heal broken relationships by making amends.

Tenth Commitment: *I will not covet the lives of others; I will be grateful for my own life and for life itself.* I will be grateful each day for who I am and what I have, and I will not diminish my human value by comparing myself to others.

Not even the strictest adherence to the ten commitments can produce a perfect life. Sadness and disappointment are part of living. Like all other people I am subject to negative thoughts and intentions. I can be fearful, angry, jealous and resentful. Sometimes I am frustrated, and I can doubt my self-worth. I may want to take revenge against people who I think have wronged me. And despite my many years of sobriety I experience moments when I feel like throwing up my hands and acting out. But *the ten commitments help me not to act on negative feelings such as these.* Even when we don't feel like doing so, the ten commitments remind us to do our best to act decently, purposefully and compassionately.

Twelve Step wisdom encourages people who seek to diminish the maladies of their soul to have a program "just for today," even if they do not follow it exactly. None of us is perfect, and I certainly do not practice the ten commitments perfectly. The only thing that I have done perfectly for the last nearly thirty years is to abstain from the use of alcohol and addictive drugs. But the daily presence of the ten commitments in my life helps me pursue the next right action, create less chaos, and find my way back to wholeness after my mistakes.

GRAINS OF SAND

The spiritual traditions of Judaism and Alcoholics Anonymous teach me that no matter how much spiritual growth we achieve, we remain lifelong works in progress. They also teach me that though we may never reach our spiritual goals, we are not therefore free to ignore them. We fulfill our spiritual mission when we do our best each day to act a grain of sand more decently, purposefully and compassionately than we did the day before.

As an imperfect human being, I accept that even this modest goal may on many days go unfulfilled. I didn't change from a hopeless addict and felon to a decent human being overnight, and I do not expect that this (or any other book) will change your life overnight either. But with the help of the ten commitments, each of us can enjoy a richer and more meaningful life one day at a time. Even if we missed the mark yesterday and screwed up today, tomorrow is another chance to do better.

YOU MATTER

One of the biggest lies that we human beings tell ourselves is that we don't matter. The process of recovering from the unique maladies of our soul begins with recognizing that we matter to ourselves and to others. When I was committing felonies and slowly killing my body and my spirit with alcohol and drugs, I told myself that I was junk, that I was powerless to change and that my life didn't matter. Those were lies. I mattered even when my life was in tatters through the chaos that I created, the damage that I did to my victims' lives and to my own soul, and the fear and anguish that I created for my family.

We matter when we refuse to compare our insides to other peoples' outsides. Even people who from the outside seem to "have it made" may create chaos by lying to themselves that they don't matter. Sid Caesar for example was the most successful television comedian of the 1950's. On his weekly network TV shows Caesar entertained huge audiences and earned millions of dollars by creating and portraying wacky characters. But as Caesar confessed many years later to a journalist, "Offstage, with my real personality for all to see, I was a mess…I couldn't believe that anyone could like me for myself." For more than twenty years, Caesar's belief that he didn't matter apart from the characters he portrayed led to depression and addiction to drugs and alcohol. At his bottom, Caesar didn't leave his house for months at a time and rarely got out of bed. He finally went into treatment and got sober. "I had to choose between life and death," Caesar told the journalist. "I chose life."

Each of us has the power to decide each day to choose life. We can live as a blessing to ourselves, our families and our communities by doing our best to live decently, act righteously, respect the dignity of others, and illuminate the darkness. We are also capable of living as a curse, hiding from the light and telling ourselves that life is unfair and that our actions don't matter.

If you are willing to choose life, the ten commitments will help you enjoy a richer and more meaningful life. You are unique, and you matter in a way that no one else does. In the Jewish tradition, a Torah scroll is not complete if even one letter is missing or damaged. In the same way, the world is not complete until you take the seat at the table that is yours alone to occupy. I hope that the ten commitments help you choose life and find your seat at the table.

A BRIEF OVERVIEW

My spiritual program of recovery from the maladies of our souls unfolds in this book as follows:

Chapter Two describes the lifestyle that landed me in prison twice, the miracle of Harriet Rossetto entering into my life, and the founding and growth of Beit T'Shuvah. I hope this background helps you better appraise the ten commitments and evaluate their application to your personal circumstances.

Chapters Three through Twelve each focus on one of the ten commitments. You will find in the chapters, in addition to discussions of the commitments and tools for practicing them, the following features:

- A Torah *drash*. The Torah is the foundation of all Jewish laws and traditions. (The Torah also constitutes the first five books of the Christian Bible.) The five books of the Torah are divided into fifty-two weekly *parshas*. A *drash* is a short teaching based on one of those *parshas*. Each chapter includes at least one *drash* that relates my understanding of a *parsha* to a commitment.
- Occasional *Rabbi Mark's App Store* segments elaborate on tools that help me to carry out the commitments.
- *Shares from the Shuv.* "The Shuv" is an affectionate nickname by which residents and alumni often refer to Beit T'Shuvah. In the Twelve Step world, "shares" are personal stories through which people discuss their experience, strength, and hope with each other. Each chapter includes a section called *Shares from the Shuv* that provides personal experiences relating to the commitment that the chapter discusses. The named contributors of the *Shares from the Shuv* include current and former residents of Beit T'Shuvah, as well as congregants and other members of the Beit T'Shuvah community. When a share's author is "A Friend," a story is a composite that doesn't represent the experiences of any single individual but illuminates the range of spiritual maladies for which people have sought recovery.

Finally, a brief Appendix sets forth my version of the "Holiness Code," a name commonly given to the expansive set of rules set out in the book of the Bible called Leviticus.

A TORAH DRASH

Keeping Our Promises to Ourselves

The *parsha Va'era* translates to "appeared." The term relates to the different places in the Torah in which God appeared. God makes a number of promises to human beings in this portion. The first promise is that we will be brought out of bondage. This promise teaches me that slavery can end, that it is not our natural state of being. Many of us are accustomed to being in bondage to maladies of the soul such as addictive behaviors, low self-esteem, and dependence on others for our happiness. This promise reminds us that we don't have to remain in bondage forever.

The second promise is that we will be delivered from bondage. This promise teaches me that we can change. We can stop lying to ourselves about the inevitability of our situations. We can stop imprisoning our souls within iron gates of our own making. This promise assures us that we can open these gates and release ourselves from self-imposed bondage.

The third promise is that we will be redeemed. This promise teaches me that none of us has to be forever defined by our past mistakes. We can't undo the past but each moment brings with it a new opportunity to choose life and live as a blessing.

The fourth promise is that we are God's people. This promise teaches me that none of us can escape the bondage of the maladies of our souls by ourselves, and that none of us has to. We are all Divine souls, and when we live in community rather than in isolation we can heal by showing compassion to each other. Compassion is the opposite of bondage. We can be compassionate with ourselves and heal old wounds, and we can show compassion to others and help them heal from their wounds.

The fifth promise is that we will be brought to our land. This promise teaches me that "our land" is not a geographical space. Each of us is brought to our land when we value our uniqueness, and our opportunity to fill a spiritual role in the world that is ours alone to fulfill. When we are brought to our land we are free to be who we really are. We can live our authentic lives, imperfectly and with compassion and respect for human dignity.

Rabbi Mark's App Store
Three Up, Three Down

A simple thought experiment teaches me that I am enough: I think of three life-affirming character traits (such as refusal to give up on people) that help me to act decently and with respect for the dignity of all people, and of three spiritually destructive traits of character (such as impatience) that can lead me to become a source of chaos and despair. The thought experiment reminds me that while events are often beyond my power to control, I am enough because all that I need to act decently or badly in reaction to events is within me. It is up to me to choose life.

SHARES FROM THE SHUV: A RICHER AND MORE MEANINGFUL LIFE

Finding My Way
Luke C.

I was an alcoholic and drug addict who was unable to stay sober even though I had been a resident of many addiction treatment facilities. My father was a Lutheran minister, and as a child I enjoyed going to church with him. Beit T'Shuvah was my first real exposure to Judaism.

I had pretty much given up on myself by the time I arrived at Beit T'Shuvah. For the first six months I was shut down. I hardly said anything to anybody and I felt spiritually dead. I finally told Rabbi Mark how hard it was for me to communicate with counselors and other residents. He asked me, "What is it that you want to say?" I replied, "I want people to know that I'm a stand-up guy." Rabbi Mark told me, "You don't have to say that. You're an addict, so no one would believe you anyway. You can be the loudest guy in the room without saying a word. Show people that you are a stand-up guy through your actions. It takes longer, but your actions will tell people who you are."

Though many people at Beit T'Shuvah had told me to "just act like a *mensch*," this conversation with Rabbi Mark was my "moment of clarity." I finally internalized the idea that my actions can communicate the message that I am a decent human being. I don't have to say that I am decent; I am decent when I pursue decent actions.

Paradoxically, this conversation with Rabbi Mark also unlocked my tongue. I no longer found it difficult to talk to people. I became a counselor at Beit T'Shuvah, but I never forgot that I can best help other addicts recover through my actions rather than my words. I met the love of my life Rachel at Beit T'Shuvah, and we got married on the beach in a small ceremony conducted by my father and Rabbi Mark. For today, I have an amazing life beyond my deserving.

Cooking for Life
Brandon B.

I paroled out of state prison to Beit T'Shuvah after doing time for using, manufacturing and selling methamphetamine. Soon after I became a resident, Rabbi Mark asked the people in one of my groups, "What do you already know how to do that you can do just a little bit differently so that you can be decent and productive?" I thought to myself, "As a meth manufacturer, I was known in the drug trade as a cook. And as a cook, what I know how to do is follow a recipe."

So I began doing what I already knew how to do a little bit differently by joining with another resident of the house to start a catering business and prepare meals for the residents of Beit T'Shuvah. My role as a cook helped me understand Rabbi Heschel's teaching that something sacred is at stake in all human activities. I saw that I was doing more than providing food. I was contributing to the wonder of residents' days, and helping them be grateful and amazed for their lives. I communicated through my actions that the residents had a seat at the table (literally) and that they mattered. And for the first time in my life I mattered by acting decently in service to others.

A day at a time, I do my best to matter and live with purpose by seeing the wonder in everyday acts of decency and kindness. And people have developed enough trust and faith in me that my job today is to interview and evaluate people who want to become residents of Beit T'Shuvah. I could not have imagined this a few years ago.

Hide and Don't Seek
Paul B.

During one of the first Friday night services that I attended at Beit T'Shuvah, Rabbi Mark talked about how healing the maladies of our souls can help all of us, even non-addicts like me, live a richer and more meaningful life.

His comments awakened in me memories of an incident from my childhood that had negatively affected my self-esteem for decades.

When I was about seven years old, I had played a game of hide-and-seek with a group of friends. Though I had often played this game with these same friends, on this particular occasion I had found a great hiding place. Such a great hiding place in fact that I stayed there for many minutes without being discovered by the player who was "It." When I finally crawled out from my hiding place voluntarily and triumphantly revealed myself, I realized that the person who had been "It" was no longer trying to find me. My friends had started a new round of hide-and-seek without me. I turned and walked home alone without saying goodbye to anyone.

Rabbi Mark's remarks about maladies other than addiction helped me understand that I was sad because I felt that I didn't matter even to my good friends. The reverberating clang of that isolated feeling had stayed with me all through school and into my adulthood. A sense that I didn't matter and wasn't good enough had undermined many of my personal and professional relationships. I often chose to hide by declining invitations to social activities such as school reunions. And when I did attend events, I often hid on the periphery, thinking that I wasn't worth the time it would take other people to get to know me. I even developed a great "hiding trick" to use when I was alone at social functions. I would stand off to the side, holding two glasses of soda or sparking water (though I'm not an addict, even before coming to Beit T'Shuvah I hardly ever drank alcohol). That way people would think that I was waiting for somebody to join me and would be less likely to approach me or feel sorry for me.

Rabbi Mark's comments taught me that spiritual healing isn't just for alcoholics or drug addicts. Though I have had a good life, it had been diminished by my discomfort in social situations. While my inclination still may be to stay on the sidelines, Rabbi Mark's approach to living well has helped me to stop hiding and to act as if I believe I am a person worth talking to.

CHAPTER TWO

BEIT T'SHUVAH

C HAPTER ONE BRIEFLY summarized my journey from addicted felon to spiritual leader of Beit T'Shuvah. So that you can better evaluate the principles of the ten commitments and their meaning for your own life, this chapter delves more deeply into my story and that of Beit T'Shuvah. I hope that the experiences that I describe in this chapter help you realize that all of us can change and that while none of us will ever do things perfectly, each day brings new opportunity to act with a grain of sand more decency, purpose and appreciation for life than we did the day before.

TOWARDS THE ABYSS

I realized that I was in desperate need of spiritual help to stay sober and live decently as I sat handcuffed in the back seat of LAPD Officer Bashira's police car. It was 1986, and for the second time in six years, Officer Bashira had arrested me for bank fraud. I eventually pled guilty and was sentenced to serve fifty-two months in California's Chino State Prison. At the time of my 1986 arrest, I had been out on parole for barely a year after serving an earlier eighteen-month term in Chino for a different series of frauds. As I sat in Officer Bashira's police car a second time I had what participants in Alcoholics Anonymous often call a "moment of clarity." I decided that I no longer wanted to throw away my life. I looked into my future, and realized that I didn't have far to see. If I couldn't figure out how to reclaim my sanity and sobriety and live as a decent human being, I would surely die in prison. And soon.

I had been wandering aimlessly in a desert of my own making for over two decades before I arrived at that moment of clarity. My descent into the abyss of addiction and crime began when I was a sixteen-year-old high school student living in Cleveland. My father, of blessed memory, was the family's sole breadwinner, and he died suddenly and unexpectedly. My mother and her three children were suddenly thrust into poverty.

I was a fat kid with few friends and little sense of self-worth, so I decided that the best way for me to contribute to family finances was to work for a local "fence," selling stolen goods on commission. My headquarters was a dingy tavern whose bartender was more than happy to sell booze to teenagers. I went to college for a year to please my mother, but spent most of my time running a crooked gambling operation before dropping out. For the next few years, I devoted my days to defrauding car dealers, banks and insurance companies and my nights to defrauding my soul in bars with women, booze and drugs. Eventually my activities brought me into conflict with higher-ups in the Cleveland mob. They were kind enough to give me a choice. I could stay in Cleveland and be killed, or I could leave town. In one of my saner moments from that period of my life, I chose the latter option.

I had a brother living in Los Angeles, so I decided on a change of scenery from snow to palm trees. Since L.A. also had banks, cars, bars and drugs, the change of scenery did not require a change of lifestyle. Scamming suckers was all I knew how to do, and I was a good enough thief to support an ever-increasing dependence on alcohol and drugs and a need to fool people into thinking I was a big shot.

My life careened out of control. I was usually too wasted to care about covering my tracks, and eventually the cops caught up to me and arrested me for passing phony checks. I made bail and in a characteristic display of *chutzpah*, supported myself while out on bail by selling stolen merchandise and passing more bad checks. Miraculously, my guilty plea resulted in probation rather than incarceration. The catch was that in order to stay on probation, I had to pay back part of the many thousands of dollars I had stolen at the rate of $500 a month. I made the first payment immediately by handing the probation officer a bad check, then headed to a nearby bar. For the next few years I continued to support myself by defrauding banks and car dealers. I was repeatedly arrested, but each time I showed up in court I managed to tell a believable enough phony hardship story to convince judges not to terminate my probation. But in 1984 my luck and my excuses ran out. I was arrested by Officer Bashira and charged with bank fraud. I pleaded guilty and was sentenced to three years in California State Prison in Chino. I was released on parole after serving eighteen months.

Prison scares some people straight. But prison made me even more crooked—if not a better crook, at least a more frantic one. During the year that I was out on parole, my life was a chaotic blur of stolen cars, bad checks, booze, and drugs. Again I was too busy committing crimes to cover my tracks. I was so disconnected from the reality of my life that I was surprised to find Officer Bashira waiting for me on a street corner one fine December afternoon in 1986. For a second time, she helped me into the back seat of her police car. I will always be grateful to her, because that car was the scene of my epiphany. (You can read a lot more about my life as a drunken gangster wannabe in my autobiography, *The Holy Thief.*)

HARRIET ROSSETTO

Around the time that I was experiencing my epiphany, Harriet Rossetto was trying to find a purpose for her life. Harriet was an unemployed Los Angeles social worker. She was not an addict; the maladies of her soul were different from mine. Her moment of clarity occurred when she read a "Help Wanted" ad placed in a newspaper for "a person of Jewish background and culture to help incarcerated Jewish offenders." It was as if the job had her name on it! She answered the ad and got the job, never imagining how much it would change her life. (Harriet tells the story of her own journey in her memoir, *Sacred Housekeeping.*)

THE HOUSE ON LAKE STREET

Harriet decided to focus on Jewish criminal offenders with addiction issues. (Few if any Jewish community leaders at the time acknowledged that such people even existed, an attitude that is still all-too-common today.) Harriet wanted ex-cons to have a place to live and heal upon their release from jails and prisons. Harriet cobbled together enough money through grants from the Jewish Community Foundation and F.E.M.A. (the Federal Emergency Management Agency) to buy an old and rapidly deteriorating Victorian house on Lake Street near downtown L.A. She turned it into a halfway house that she called Beit T'Shuvah, Hebrew for House of Return (or Turning). The initial occupants were Harriet and three former prisoners who, on their first night in the house, stole from Harriet's room the few pieces of jewelry that she owned.

The humble, drug-and-crime-ridden neighborhood was not the best locale for a community of addicts trying to stay sober. The local street dealers learned, like others before them, how persuasive Harriet could be. She convinced them to promise not to solicit her residents, and for the most part they lived up to their promises. Some years later, the police asked for permission to use the attic of the Lake Street house as a lookout post that officers could use to detect illegal drug dealing on the streets below. As much as we understood the destructive power of illegal drugs, we did not give the police access to the attic. The locals had acted with decency towards us, and if the police were to succeed in reducing the level of criminal activity on Lake Street they would have to do it without help from us.

Lake Street was a "double halfway house." It was halfway between incarceration and freedom, and halfway between building and rubble. Though the house provided little more than "three hots and a cot" for about twenty-five residents squeezed into a few bedrooms, for Harriet it was heaven. She set about visiting L.A.-area Jewish inmates with substance abuse issues. She told them about Beit T'Shuvah, and invited them to check it out when they were released. One of Harriet's trips brought her to Chino State Prison, and it was there that I first met her. Admittedly, it was an unlikely place for a first date.

When I paroled out of prison for a second time, my prospects for avoiding a third trip to prison hovered between slim and none. I was sober and I had devoted a lot of time while in prison to studying Jewish texts and attending Alcoholics Anonymous meetings. Nevertheless I was a two-time loser with no college degree, no driver's license, no job and no legitimate job skills. I wanted to change my life but I had no idea about how I could get from where I was to somewhere else. I felt like I had lived the title of Richard Fariña's marvelous novel, *Been Down So Long It Looks Like Up To Me*. I didn't know if a pathway to "up" from where I was existed, or how to find the pathway if it did. But after about two weeks into my parole and with nothing else going on in my life, I remembered Harriet's visit and took a bus to the Lake Street house and rang the bell.

HARRIET AND MARK

When Harriet answered the door I explained to her that I was in desperate need of a job and that I was willing to start working immediately. Harriet pointed to piles of what looked like junk to me and said that if I was willing

14

to work a part-time minimum wage job, I could set up a thrift shop in an empty side room. I was thrilled to have any sort of job, so I accepted the offer and began to organize and display the used bric-a-brac with the same zeal as if I were about to sell diamonds in a new branch of Tiffany's.

Now that I was connected to a Jewish faith-based house of recovery, I wanted to continue the spiritual growth that I had begun to experience in prison. As I mentioned in Chapter One, during my second prison stretch I had attended Alcoholics Anonymous meetings and studied Jewish texts. I had noticed that though their principles and traditions seemed very different on the surface, Judaism and Alcoholics Anonymous had a lot in common. Both offered spiritual paths to decency through self-examination, connection to community, service to others and commitment to a spiritual force for good that is greater than any individual. I suggested to Harriet that we add a spiritual component to Beit T'Shuvah's recovery program by holding Friday night services that combined the spiritual traditions of Judaism and Alcoholics Anonymous. Even though Harriet had long disassociated herself from religious observances, she readily agreed to my proposal. Friday night services for residents and family members who wanted to join them, as well as other addicts, became a bi-weekly Beit T'Shuvah activity. I conducted the services in a tent set up in the backyard, and we talked every week about applying the spiritual principles of Judaism and A.A. to our own circumstances so that we could maintain sobriety and live decently.

While I still struggled with my own sobriety, I began to understand that I had the capacity to act righteously. For the first time in my adult life I was taking responsibility for my actions instead of blaming my problems on bad luck or somebody else's stupidity. I wasn't thinking about what I would do for the rest of my life. I was satisfied to wake up each morning with a sense of decent purpose.

When Harriet's assistant relapsed, I turned my thrift store duties over to another resident and became her new assistant. Together Harriet and I became a team, speaking to school groups and trying to raise money from Jewish community groups. I was still a street hustler, but now I saw myself as "hustling for God." And for Harriet—we got married in 1990.

RABBI MARK

As Beit T'Shuvah became more entrenched in the community, Harriet and I realized that I needed more than my street smarts if I was to be taken seriously by the donors from whom we solicited contributions. I took night college courses, graduating with a B.A. degree in 1995. That is when I also began studying Torah each week with the man who to this day remains my spiritual mentor, Rabbi Ed Feinstein. Ed is a rabbi at Valley Beth Shalom, one of L.A.'s largest and most socially active Jewish congregations. Our weekly meetings were always more like sparring sessions, because Ed's formal training in the interpretation of the Torah and other Jewish texts was grounded in books while mine was grounded in the streets.

Once I had earned a B.A., Harriet and Ed urged me to go on to rabbinical school. I was reluctant, only partly because I wasn't sure of the enthusiasm with which a rabbinical school would welcome an application from a two-time ex-con and recovering addict. In addition, I'd be almost fifty years old when (and if) I got my degree. Rabbinical school would also mean another four years of sleep-deprivation, because I'd still have to work at Beit T'Shuvah in order to afford the tuition payments. Finally the whole student thing—sitting in classes, taking notes, writing papers—wasn't really me. I could barely sit still for five minutes. But I did apply and I was thrilled when I was accepted. I stuck it out and in the year 2000, to the amazement of many who knew me from the streets or from prison, I became a real rabbi.

GROWTH AND COMMITMENT

To the chagrin of many former residents who had "made their bones" (to borrow a term from *The Godfather*) in the gritty Lake Street house, Beit T'Shuvah moved a few miles west to a much larger (though still modest) building around the time that I became a rabbi. The move provided the space for Beit T'Shuvah to become a synagogue as well as a larger residential addiction treatment facility, which today houses, feeds and rehabilitates about one hundred male and female residents. Through the years Beit T'Shuvah has earned a national reputation for providing effective treatment for a variety of addictions, with residents coming from all across the U.S. and Canada, and sometimes from other countries as well.

But just as when Harriet first opened its doors, Beit T'Shuvah continues to serve former inmates, and many of its residents pay little or nothing for care and treatment. At the same time, Harriet and I are committed to never turning away an addict who is willing to ask for help and work our program. The traditions of Judaism and Alcoholics Anonymous teach us that no one is hopeless, and that every soul is worth fighting for. We want Beit T'Shuvah to be a sanctuary for all people, from any background and from all faiths or from none at all, who feel lost and empty. Every soul can heal. To the best of our ability, no one who is sentenced to, or walks or crawls into, Beit T'Shuvah will be left behind.

Beit T'Shuvah's commitments to its residents extend beyond sobering them up and sending them into the world. As reflected in the ten commitments that are the foundation of Beit T'Shuvah's program, its broader mission is to help "all who enter to recover their passion and discover their purpose." For example, residents can take "surf therapy." The music program involves many residents, alumni and congregants in synagogue services and talent shows, as well as nationwide performances of *Freedom Song*, a musical play about addiction and recovery written by residents and staff. Recently the music department began a music publishing section, another outlet for creative residents in their journey of self-discovery. Many residents develop self-assurance by training for and participating in the annual L.A. Marathon. And Beit T'Shuvah's externship program gives residents a chance to learn (or re-learn) accountability and job skills while they are in treatment. Our goal is for residents to move out of "the house" with a plan that provides them with a decent daily purpose, just like me when I began organizing the Lake Street thrift shop.

According to the Biblical story of Exodus, the Jews wandered in the desert for forty years before they entered their Promised Land. Recovery from maladies of the soul is a similarly long and difficult process that I pursue a day at a time and that I will never fully achieve. I didn't leave the desert in my rear-view mirror the moment I decided to be sober and live decently. I shall have to work at recovery and decency each day. When I do the work, my reward is that I get to continue the struggle to be a grain of sand better every day.

Echoing the hope espoused by Rabbi Yohanan ben Zakkai, a second century rabbi who lived in Jerusalem during the Roman siege, the sixteenth century Protestant theologian Martin Luther taught, "Even if it looks like the end of the world is coming tomorrow, still I would plant a tree today." Rabbi Yohanan and Martin Luther teach us that no matter how bleak a situation appears to be, we can live with hope that tomorrow will be better. Whether we feel lost and broken or whether we just want to act a little bit more decently tomorrow than we did today, every moment is a new opportunity to commit to pursuing a richer and more meaningful life. I hope you are ready: the world needs you. The world needs all of us.

I am not at peace. I will never be at peace as long as a single human being feels that he or she doesn't matter. May Beit T'Shuvah remain forever a sanctuary for anyone who feels lost and empty. And please God, may it someday be unnecessary for Beit T'Shuvah to exist.

A TORAH DRASH

For or Against

The *parsha Korach* tells the story of a rebellion by a leader named Korach who was dissatisfied with his role in the life of the Israelites. He accused Moses and Aaron of putting themselves above the people. Yet at the same time he demanded to be the High Priest and thus above the people. Korach was able to convince himself that he was right to condemn others for doing what he wanted to do.

The Korach story reminds me to ask myself whether I am just an "anti," rebelling *against* something, or if I am rebelling *for* something. Martin Luther King Jr. didn't simply rebel against an existing order or legal prejudice. He led a rebellion *for* human dignity; he rebelled *for* the right of people of all races, colors, creeds and religions to liberty, justice and happiness. My wife Harriet Rossetto rebelled *for* the dignity of the human spirit when she struggled to create a shelter for Jewish addicts who had nowhere to go after their release from prisons and jails, and she continues to rebel *for* all who seek to overcome the maladies of their souls so they can better realize their passions and purposes. When I rebel *for* something I am passionate and non-defensive. When I "rebel *for*," I am able to incorporate the ideas and beliefs of others who seek to create a better world. I don't have to prove anything; I am blessed to share my vision with others. This is the way that Moses and Aaron responded to Korach and his rebellion. When I "rebel *for*," I can enhance my life and the life of the community.

SHARES FROM THE SHUV: A HOUSE OF HEALING

Paying it Forward
Carrie N.

I was blessed with the opportunity to be a resident of Beit T'Shuvah when "the house" (as we called it) was on Lake Street. With three felony cases pending, and two reluctant judges intent on sending me to state prison, Rabbi Mark was somehow able to work magic and convince them to allow me one last chance to get my life together.

Fast forward to a Friday afternoon a few months later when I walked up those infamous Lake Street steps. Initially I was a bit taken aback by the dilapidated house that was to be my home for the next year. But by the time I was welcomed at what would be the first of many Shabbos celebrations, I began to feel the magic that was Lake Street. And it was in that house where I learned to live, not from a place of negativity and fear, but from my soul. More than anything, Beit T'Shuvah is where I learned about living based on spiritual principles and what I can do for others, rather than "what's in it for me."

Ultimately, Harriet and Rabbi bestowed upon me the greatest blessing of all when they offered me the opportunity to do the work that was at the heart of how Beit T'Shuvah came to be. In 1999, I was able to begin working with Jewish inmates in local jails and state prisons. They gave me the opportunity to do for others what others had done for me.

Today I oversee an entire department that is dedicated to reaching out to Jewish men and women who have found themselves ensnared in the criminal justice system. And, while the "official" undertaking of the Alternative Sentencing department is to assess individuals who want to become residents of Beit T'Shuvah, it is the spiritual mission that is the most meaningful to me. Through face-to-face visits at the local jails as well as through correspondence with inmates in prisons, both in California and throughout the country, I have found purpose and passion in carrying the message of recovery and the teachings of Beit T'Shuvah to those who are behind the gates and walls of our penal institutions.

One of the things I have learned about myself on my own journey of recovery is that I am a fighter. When I first walked up the steps to Lake Street that was not necessarily an asset. But as Rabbi Mark taught me long ago, if we work at it we can take our character defects, flip them on their head, and learn how to use them for good. To this end I have made it my mission to fight for second chances for my clients who are deserving of them. And, one of the areas where I have done my most rewarding fighting is in advocating for the release of life inmates who have been imprisoned for twenty or thirty years, usually for their involvement in a crime where a life was lost. Despite many of my lifers having received decades-old sentences that included the promise of a chance to earn their release through rehabilitation, for most lifers the tough-on-crime legislation and ballot propositions in subsequent years eliminated virtually all hope of release. For twenty plus years, California lifers were denied parole out of hand, without consideration of the circumstances of their crime, their specific part in it, or of any positive transformation they may have made during the course of their incarceration.

I have fought for many lifers over the years, men and women who are deserving of a second chance. I can still remember the moment that I got word that my first lifer was going to be allowed to parole: I was screaming so loud in the hallways of Beit T'Shuvah my colleagues thought I had lost my mind! In December of 2006, after being incarcerated for twenty-four years for her part in a robbery in which the victim was killed, this former lifer who has become my friend was finally able to come home. She ultimately became a counselor at Beit T'Shuvah and she has been able, like me, to "pay it forward" and help others recover from their emotional and spiritual maladies. Since that time, more of "my" lifers have come home. Their recovery and service to others inspire me to be a better me and to work harder at what I do.

I have celebrated more than twenty years of sobriety. I will celebrate in the rooms of Alcoholics Anonymous by taking cakes and thanking my sponsor, my sobriety sisters, and the fellowship. But the most special and meaningful celebrations occur when I take my cakes at Beit T'Shuvah on Friday night Shabbat services. Not only do I love being able to see the many clients I have connected with over the years take their cakes, but Beit T'Shuvah is, for me, the heart and soul of my recovery. Beit T'Shuvah is where I grew up and learned how to love, how to give, and how to live. More than anything, I consider myself fortunate to be able to work here every day, where I am surrounded by recovery and love. Thank you Beit T'Shuvah for a life beyond my wildest dreams.

Accepting My Addictions
Jeremy P.

I am not Jewish, but Beit T'Shuvah is my "blessing with an address." I have been in and out of gangs and the criminal justice system since before I was a teenager. I have seen some of the darkest corners of the human spirit. The statistics say that I should not have made it out. But now that I am in recovery at Beit T'Shuvah, I have made the choice to walk a different path and I work as a program facilitator.

When I was eleven years old my older brother had an accident that left him handicapped. I started to act out both in school and at home. I began using marijuana, which led to my first run-in with the law, and by the age of thirteen I had been jumped into a gang. I became violent and angry, especially after one of my homies was shot and died in my arms. I couldn't feel empathy or joy; I was numb, except for the rage. I left home when I was sixteen years old and supported myself by gangbanging and selling drugs. By the time I was twenty I was using heroin. It was the first time in my life that the weight of my miserable life vanished. But it wasn't long before I was arrested and convicted of possession. Since it was my first offense, the drug court judge gave me a suspended sentence. I wouldn't have to do time as long as I stayed clean.

Back on the streets, I went right back to using. Two weeks away from completing my suspended sentence, the cops caught me with heroin again. When I went back to court I asked the judge to continue my suspended sentence and send me to Beit T'Shuvah instead of state prison. The judge refused, and sentenced me to thirty-two months in prison. Three weeks later the judge had a change of heart. The judge ordered me back to court and offered me a chance to go to Beit T'Shuvah. I guess I wasn't committed yet to changing my life, because I asked the judge to give me a week to think it over. The judge told me that I was a knucklehead, and he gave me two seconds to make a decision. I looked over at my mom, and said, "Yes." At age twenty-four, I came to Beit T'Shuvah for the first time.

Still I didn't truly accept that I was an addict. I had one foot in recovery and one foot out. I stayed at Beit T'Shuvah for seven months, then left against the advice of my treatment team. They were right. Within a month, I was arrested again and convicted of possessing and selling heroin. This time there was no miracle phone call from a judge. I was sentenced to three years in prison.

But something changed in my mind while I was in prison. I decided that I wanted to live differently, and I got the chance to when I was released from prison early and accepted back as a resident of Beit T'Shuvah. This time around I have completely surrendered. I am ready at last to change my life and live decently. Whatever I am asked to do, I am willing. I am a performer in the Beit T'Shuvah original musical play *Freedom Song*, and I attend meetings of Criminals and Gang Members Anonymous. During the closing prayer at many Friday night Sabbath services, I perform an original rap that I wrote. And I have allowed myself to be vulnerable. For the first time in my life I am living decently and with daily purpose.

I have also grown spiritually. I once thought that the only thing bigger than me was my neighborhood. Now I accept that a power greater than me exists and can help me to live clean. I now look forward to going to work and learning. And I feel good about helping people, instead of taking from them and hurting them. My family is proud of me and they support me. My mother cried when she saw a recording of me performing in *Freedom Song*. And now I am married to Lindsay, an alumna of "the house." We are the parents of a lovely son, and sometimes I hold him while I rap during the closing prayer. A day at a time, my life is amazing.

CHAPTER THREE

FIRST COMMITMENT

I will understand God in a way that helps me to act righteously.

THE BIBLE'S FIRST Commandment states, "I am the Lord your God, who brought you out of the land of Egypt, out of the house of bondage. You shall have no other gods before me." I understand the commandment as imposing an obligation on human beings to live as a righteous representative of a single and supreme, eternal God. By linking this obligation to God's freeing people from bondage, the commandment teaches me to represent God through actions rather than through statements, feelings, intentions or beliefs. We reflect our obligation to God by doing our best to *act* righteously.

My corollary first spiritual commitment is to understand God in a way that helps me to act righteously. Many people develop an understanding of God through an "outside in" process of religious education. My understanding of God by contrast results from an "inside out" process of spiritual experience. The relevant question for me is not "What is the meaning of God?" but rather is "How can I personally understand God in a way that helps me each day to do my best to act righteously?"

AN INNER SPARK OF HOLINESS

Throughout the ages, people have understood the concept of God in an infinite variety of ways. Certainly a god of any form was not part of my life during the two decades that I lived as an addicted felon. I hid from my own soul, and my life during that time was a train wreck.

Over the course of my immersion in the texts and traditions of Judaism and Alcoholics Anonymous, I have come to understand my need for a connection to a power greater than myself in order to stay sober and act righteously. I have also come to understand that, whatever meaning the concept of God may have for other people, I have the power and indeed the obligation to develop an understanding of God that helps me *personally* to enjoy a richer and more meaningful life by acting righteously and living with daily purpose and passion for life.

I fulfill my first commitment by understanding God (or my higher or greater power) as *an inner spark of holiness*. This inner spark, which represents my soul or my conscience, is the source of an impulse to act righteously. And as the First Commandment's concept of a single God teaches me, the same spark of holiness exists within all other human beings. This conception of my higher power helps me to act righteously because it teaches me that I am a holy soul, that all other people are holy souls, and that within all of us exists an impulse to act righteously. This first commitment is therefore the foundation of spiritual buoyancy. It reminds me that all human beings are kinfolk to me, and that something more enduring and important than my personal satisfaction is at stake in every action I take.

My understanding of God as an inner spark of holiness means that my higher power does not exist in events but rather through my righteous actions in response to events. I do not blame God for natural disasters or human suffering, nor do I bestow credit on God for human achievement. Instead, I thank my inner spark of holiness for the power to choose to act righteously in response to what is good and bad in the world. When natural disasters occur or tyrants or terrorists create suffering, I reflect my inner spark when I do what I can to help the victims. When I enjoy success, I act as a holy soul when I share the fruits of my success with others. When I experience loss or disappointment, I act righteously when I continue to hold on to my principles. Whatever external events beset or delight me, my impulse to act righteously helps me to act decently in response to those events.

In the Jewish tradition, creation is not limited to a single and ancient "Big Bang" moment of time. Instead, creation is a continuous process. This tradition also promotes spiritual buoyancy because it teaches me that no matter the mistakes and misdeeds of the past, with each new moment our inner spark of holiness is pure and good. Our inner spark gives us the opportunity to re-create ourselves and renew our lives at each moment. No matter how we have lived in the past, our impulse to act righteously survives and allows us to start to act more decently today.

I cannot rationally understand or describe the ultimate power and focus of worship that God has represented throughout history and within diverse cultures, religions and sects. I recognize that the role (if any) of a God or a higher power of any form in one's life is among our most personal and often private decisions. Connection to a higher power is not a necessary component of a commitment to act righteously, nor does profession of belief in a higher power necessarily produce righteous actions. You may not relate to this first commitment either because you perceive no need to connect to a higher power in order to live a richer and more meaningful life, or because your conception of a higher power is very different from mine. If so, I invite you to follow the Twelve Step wisdom to "take what you like and leave the rest." Whether or not connection to a higher power of any type stimulates you to act with compassion for the poor, the widow, the orphan and the stranger, you can nevertheless act with compassion for the poor, the widow, the orphan and the stranger.

GET TO'S AND HAVE TO'S

This first commitment obligates me to do my best to reflect my impulse to act righteously in my daily life. I realize that many people chafe at the idea of obligations, regarding them as "things I have to do that I don't want to do." But for me, an obligation to act righteously as a representative of an eternal higher power is a source of satisfaction and joy because obligation converts *have to's* into *get to's*. I don't *have to* act righteously by giving *tzedakah* (donations of money or property) and sharing what I have with others. My obligation to give *tzedakah* creates spiritual buoyancy because I *get to* act righteously by sharing my blessings with others. I don't *have to* act righteously by making amends for my mistakes; I am joyful because I *get to* act in accord with the holiness of my soul by making amends and repairing old wounds. I don't *have to* do what I can to help those who are ill or infirm feel that they matter; I *get to* demonstrate to people who are ill or infirm (or to their families) that they matter. And I don't *have to* act with care and concern for future generations, I *get to* add my righteous actions to the legacy of the past and present that passes to those who come after me. By transforming *have-to's* into *get-to's*, an obligation to act righteously that flows from the first commitment becomes a source of satisfaction and spiritual buoyancy rather than a basis of resentment.

EVERYDAY HOLINESS

I grew up believing that holiness was a quality that was beyond the reach of ordinary people like me. I equated holiness with perfection and thought of it as the exclusive province of saints, religious leaders and those few who were blessed with an ability to interpret the will of a distant and unknowable Divine power with a certainty that I lacked.

But my understanding of my higher power as an inner spark of holiness that provides me with an impulse to act righteously means that holiness has nothing to do with perfection, religious doctrine or belief or with Divine certainty. Instead, we reflect our holiness whenever our actions demonstrate decency, compassion, and respect for our own dignity and the dignity of others. This is so important! When I recognize that I am a holy soul who dwells in a world filled with holy souls, every life-affirming action I take, whether it consists of comforting a friend or smiling at a passerby, creates a moment of spiritual goodness. We are holy when we act with kindness and compassion. We are holy when we celebrate another person's achievement or send someone a note of appreciation for a good deed or for simply being a friend. We are holy when we are empathic, acknowledging the imperfections in ourselves that we so readily recognize in other people. We are holy when we make amends for our mistakes. We are holy when we are joyful for the gift of life and grateful for what we have. We are holy when we are unwilling to take unfair advantage of another person's ignorance or weakness.

As the spiritual leader of a residential addiction treatment center, I have been privileged to experience daily the power of the spark of holiness that exists within all people. I have seen countless numbers of people redeem seemingly hopeless lives and begin to live as decent human beings. None of us can erase the misdeeds of the past, and the consequences of past misdeeds may affect our lives and the lives of others forever. But if we cannot wipe away the past, neither can past mistakes prevent us from redeeming our lives. As our inner spark of holiness remains pure and good, we all have the capacity to recover from the maladies of our souls by acting more decently from now on. No one is hopeless. Everyone can heal. Every life matters.

One of the most powerful and poignant depictions of a redemptive "moment of clarity" occurs during the classic 1982 film *The Verdict*. In the film Frank Galvin (played by Paul Newman) is an alcoholic personal injury lawyer whose career has spiraled downwards and nearly vanished into the abyss. Galvin's sole remaining client is a woman who became comatose through the alleged negligence of two hospital anesthesiologists. To create sympathy that he hopes will result in a speedy settlement offer from the defense lawyer that will finance his alcoholism for a while longer, Galvin goes into the hospital room to take photos of his pathetic client lying in bed and kept alive by tubes and machines. After snapping a few Polaroid pictures, Galvin collapses into a bedside chair, staring silently at his client. The development of the photos mirrors Galvin's developing sense of decency and personal responsibility for his client's welfare. He spurns a quick settlement, stops drinking, and ultimately convinces a trial jury to award his client a huge amount of money that will be adequate to cover the cost of life-long care.

Whatever the maladies of our souls, the spark of holiness that exists within each of us means that we can all change, we can all live better. One day and one grain of sand at a time, each of us can use our small corner of the world to create a little more kindness, justice and joy for ourselves and for others.

IMMORTALITY

The ultimate gift of my understanding of God as an eternal inner spark of holiness is to experience occasional glimpses of immortality. The impulse to choose to live as a blessing rather than as a curse is eternal. The spark of holiness that dwells within each of us has dwelled within the people of all the generations that preceded us and all that will follow us. When we obligate ourselves to do our best to choose life, we connect our souls to those of all other generations. And one day at a time, we can do our small part to make the world a better place for ourselves and our communities, and for all the generations that will follow us.

A TORAH DRASH 1

Where Does God Speak to Me?

The *parsha BeHar* translates to "on the mountain." The Torah tells us that this is the place where God spoke to Moses. As I read this Torah portion today I ask myself, "Where does God speak to me?" As the God of my understanding is an inner spark of holiness, God speaks to me wherever and whenever I choose to be conscious of God.

For example, God speaks to me when I can listen to others, when the concerns of others become my concerns, and when I connect to nature and human beings at the same time. And I can listen to God when I pray or meditate, when I remember the holiness of my ancestors and the holiness of those I love, and when I am open to listening to the wisdom of my soul.

I wish it were easy for us to distinguish the voice of our soul from our emotional or our intellectual voices. I am struck by how often people use the phrase "God's will" to explain the unexplainable. I don't understand why bad things happen to good people or why good things happen to not-so-good people. If I say it is God's will, that is a cop-out with which I pretend to explain what I don't understand. I don't believe that we have to explain or understand everything. Acknowledging the mystery that is life and death is important and necessary to keep ourselves right-sized. Our search for meaning in and beyond the mystery is our exciting journey of living well and listening to God. Let's not lessen the mystery with easy answers. Instead let's be willing to wrestle with the mystery and the marvel of life.

A TORAH DRASH 2

Spirituality in a Cup of Coffee

The *parsha Metzora* translates as "to the leper." In my understanding the phrase does not refer to leprosy as a permanent physical condition. Rather, the Torah addresses a physical manifestation of a spiritual malady.

This Torah portion can be difficult to write about because it does not provide a narrative story. But when I walked into my favorite coffee store not long ago I found my narrative. I ordered my usual beverage and as I waited for it, I noticed at least ten customers hurry into the store, pick up a cup of coffee that was already waiting for them, and leave. I realized that these people had pre-ordered and paid for their drinks online. What jumped out at me was the lack of human connection between the customers and the coffee store employees who had served them. For me, this is the sort of spiritual malady that turns people into *metzoras,* or lepers. When we are too busy to acknowledge the humanity of the people we interact with we take away a piece of our own humanity. And when we take the time in our everyday lives to look at people, use their names and demonstrate through our actions that we appreciate them and that they are important to us, we build up our humanity. Let us all resolve not to become *metzoras*. Let us be the *physicians of our souls* and strengthen our spiritual health by respecting the dignity and acknowledging the humanity of all people, even for seemingly mundane events such as enjoying our morning beverage.

Rabbi Mark's App Store
Acting "As If"

Acting *as if* is a tool in Twelve-Step programs that has helped many people and me foster a connection to a power greater than ourselves. Early in my recovery, I acted *as if* I was connected to a universal life force that was greater than I was and that wanted me to think of the needs of others as well as my own. Over time, my hypothetical connection to a higher power became a real one. The considerations below helped me to move from *acting as if* to *acting in connection*.

- Initially, I was willing to accept that acting *as if* would seem unnatural and artificial. In order to evaluate the helpfulness of the technique fairly, I was willing to force myself to act *as if* for a period of months.
- I sought advice from people I respected who lived decently and in connection with a power greater than themselves. While I was ultimately responsible for my own actions, insight into how other decent people connected their actions to a greater power helped me consider the value of seeking that connection in my own life.
- When acting *as if*, I thought consciously about what I would do if I were acting solely in my own interest, and what I would do if my inner spirit were reminding me to think about the needs of others as well as my own. The result might be as insignificant as a somewhat larger charitable contribution. But I was less interested in the specific results than in recognizing that a connection to a power greater than myself could affect my actions.
- I imagined private conversations between my conscience and me. Even if I wasn't Moses in the wilderness, I could still act *as if* by telling my conscience how I was feeling and what actions I was considering, and imagining my conscience's responses. These quiet and private role-play conversations helped me accept that my conscience could be a part of me and separate from me at the same time.

SHARES FROM THE SHUV: ACTING FOR GOD

The Spark Never Died
Richie K.

I was eight substances deep into my drug addiction, as well as a liar, a thief and a pusher, before I became willing to seek recovery. My brain kept telling me that I was hollow inside, and an absolutely useless piece of garbage.

Now that I am part of a recovery community, I realize that selfishness was the root cause of all my bad behavior. When I drank, used and stole, I constantly served myself and ignored others. I have slowly learned that all the time there was something intrinsically good inside of me that never deserted me no matter how hard I tried to squelch it. Despite the chaos I left in my wake, within me remained a selfless spirit that I now think of as my higher power. While I still am subject to "me first" thinking, my higher power helps me to care about other people and want to be of service to them. And I don't believe that I am alone in my struggle to take care of my needs while trying to satisfy those of other people. I think that every person who has ever lived has experienced this struggle. Knowing that my desire to be selfless emanates from a power greater than myself helps me to remain clean and sober.

Surrendering to the Right Voice
Barbara F.

When I was in the throes of my addiction, a small inner voice repeatedly told me that I was in trouble. But it was drowned out by another voice that said, "Don't worry, you got this, you're not that bad, you can always stop." I always listened to the wrong voice, like when I tried to pick up a phony prescription that I had called in myself to a pharmacy and listened to the inner voice that told me that the cop wasn't waiting there for me. As usual that voice was wrong—I got arrested.

I listened to the wrong voice for a very long time. When I finally came to Beit T'Shuvah, I knew that I had to figure out how to listen to a different voice or I would die. The different voice was that of a higher power. During the years that I was in and out of Alcoholics Anonymous, I did not connect to a higher power. I was so arrogant that on the front page of my original A.A. book I wrote, "What's the difference between God's will and Barbara's will?" I truly did not know the answer. But Beit T'Shuvah's approach to living well helped me surrender to the fact and knowledge that there *had* to be something greater than me that had brought me safely to "the house." How could I not surrender? My best thinking had landed me in jail amid shattered family relationships and financial ruin.

Today, I rely on my higher power because I know that I do not have all the answers. The life that I have now—that I *get to* have—is only a result of learning humility and gratitude and having a Higher Power in my life.

The Wrong Question
Shia B.

I am a former resident of and spiritual counselor at Beit T'Shuvah. An experience that took place during a weekly ethics class for residents produced one of the most meaningful insights of my recovery.

As it often did, the topic of the role of God or a higher power in staying sober and living decently arose during this particular ethics class. During the class, a resident asked me whether one had to believe in God to be a good person. I responded at once that of course people don't have to believe in God to be a good person. I mentioned that I know plenty of good people who don't believe in God, and that unfortunately there are many people who do all sorts of bad things in the name of God.

Friday night *Shabbat* service began shortly after this ethics class, and as it happened I was to provide a short bit of wisdom at the beginning of the service. I shared with the Beit T'Shuvah congregants my exchange with the resident, and said that on reflection a better response to the resident would have been that he had asked the wrong question. The relevant question isn't whether "people" need to believe in God to be a good person. The question we need to ask ourselves is, "Do *I personally* need to connect to God or a higher power to be a good person?" This is a question that each of us can answer for ourselves. I am still not sure of the answer for myself, but I think that my continued willingness to ask myself the question helps me to stay sober and act decently.

Soul and Science
Justin R.

The drug-use portion of my story is a lot like every other drug-user's story. It was bad, especially if you add in my Crohn's Disease. I want to focus on what came next: the good. In January 2011, I left Florida to become a day patient at Beit T'Shuvah. The first person I met when I walked in the front door told me a dirty joke. I knew I was home.

After I became a resident, I worked up the courage to tell Rabbi Mark that I was not an atheist, but that my background was in science and I was heavily agnostic. I figured that if I was to live better, logical thinking was the best way for me to get there. For a long time, my residency was a rollercoaster ride in which I tried to harmonize my inner logician with my inner spiritual self. At early morning Torah Study and other meetings, Rabbi Mark discussed Einstein and Rabbi Heschel and kept asking questions for which simple, logical answers did not exist. When I became willing to stop acting like a contrarian asshole, I embraced difficult questions that lacked "provable" answers. I cherished instead of rejected the possibility of spiritual connection as a way to live better. I reconnected with my passion for photography. I accepted that science and spirituality co-exist.

A good personal trainer will guide a bodybuilder through a process of tearing muscle fibers and push them further than they could push themselves. If I had to sum up my six-plus year relationship with Rabbi Mark with one sentence, it would be this: My soul is my muscle, and Rabbi Mark is my personal trainer.

Glenn G.
Re-Awakening My Song

Four decades of drug and alcohol abuse had wrecked my life and my song-writing career by the time I washed up on the steps of Beit T'Shuvah with a crushed spirit and only a toothbrush to my name. I didn't know if I wanted to live or die, but for reasons I don't understand I was finally willing to seek guidance. I was so glad for people to tell me what to do and when to do it because I hurt too much to think for myself.

Rabbi Mark was my spiritual counselor and he was the perfect example of the proverb, "When the student is ready, the teacher will appear." With his guidance, I acknowledged my past negativity as historical fact that no longer defined who I was. The principles of Judaism helped me to connect to a higher power that encouraged me to re-invent myself each day. Instead of using alcohol and drugs to hide from the struggle between the light and the dark, I welcomed the struggle as an opportunity to learn something new every day, and to live in truth with purpose and passion for life.

With my new identity, I was able to re-awaken my love for music. I started as an apprentice in Beit T'Shuvah's Music department, and now I am the managing director of Creative Arts and the head of an independent music publishing company. I've come to realize that my journey is a song that never ends, as one chorus after another I find ways to give back to the community with a renewed sense of obligation to live life well while helping others to live well.

Finding My Connection
Taylor Q.

My grandmother had always been there for me after my parents divorced, and her death when I was a young girl turned my world upside down. At age twelve I got jumped into a street gang and began to live a double life. I lived with my dad and his second wife, and played flute and piccolo in the school orchestra. But after school I would go out with the gang and smoke dope, fight, go tagging and steal. I was in and out of jail and Juvenile Hall, though I did manage to graduate from high school. My dad found out about my addictions and gang activities when I went to prison. When I got out of prison he refused to let me live with him.

I used drugs every day, and lived on the streets while gang banging with my homies. After one arrest I found out that I was six months pregnant, and I had a baby girl two weeks after I got out of jail. The baby's father was in prison, and when he got out I went to stay with him. But he kept beating me, and I kept stealing to support my drug habit.

When I had to go to jail again I asked my parents to take care of my daughter. I lost custody of her, and when I was finally released from jail no one would even pick me up. With nowhere to go I cried for help. I called my stepmother, she called my mother, and I ended up in Beit T'Shuvah.

I have been sober for over twenty months and now have my family, including my little girl, in my life again. I get great support from the Shuv community, I work the Twelve Steps with a sponsor who went through the house, and I attend meetings of Criminals and Gang Members Anonymous.

When I was growing up I never thought that God cared about me. Now I know that God has always been there for me, but it's up to me to hear God's voice in the wisdom of other people. I need to stay connected to God to stay sober and live decently, and I know that God acts in me through the presence of people in my life who help me see the difficult things that I can't see on my own. I work in Beit T'Shuvah's thrift store, and I feel blessed to have the life that I do now.

CHAPTER FOUR

SECOND COMMITMENT

I will diminish resentment by practicing forgiveness.

THE BIBLE'S SECOND Commandment states, "You shall not make for yourself an image in the form of anything in heaven above or on the earth beneath or in the waters below. You shall not bow down to them or serve them." I understand the commandment to mean that the power and indeed the very concept of God is so far beyond human comprehension that any tangible symbol or representation of God is necessarily false and misleading.

My corollary second spiritual commitment flows from God's behavior following the Israelites' disobedience of the second commandment. The Torah tells us that after delivering the Ten Commandments to the Israelites, Moses went back up Mt. Sinai to continue to converse with God. In his absence, the Israelites disobeyed the commandment by building and worshipping a golden calf. God's resentment of the Israelites' actions was so strong that God was ready to smite them all. God's resentment seems justifiable: after all, the Israelites violated an explicit command (and with world record speed!). But the Torah goes on to say that God's resentment was quickly replaced by forgiveness; very little smiting took place. The Jewish tradition here teaches me that resentment is a golden calf of negativity. My second commitment is to act on my impulse to act righteously by doing my best to diminish the power of resentment to control my actions through the practice of forgiveness.

RESENTMENT

Resentment is a powerful human emotion (and according to Jewish tradition, a Divine one as well). But more than an emotion, *resentment is an action* because it produces a desire to take revenge against the targets of our resentment. Among the many ways we may seek revenge are by inflicting punishment or harm on those whom we resent; by severing relationships; by engaging in hurtful gossiping; by giving people the "silent treatment" and thus communicating to them that they are "less than" and don't matter; and by speaking to people angrily or scornfully. Resentment and the urge for revenge can destroy lengthy relationships. Resentment can even tear families apart; I have experienced situations in which resentments for past mistakes prevent family members from being in a hospital room at the same time to say goodbye to a dying close relative. To paraphrase Dr. Morbius in *Forbidden Planet* (one of my all-time favorite sci-fi movies), resentment is a powerful "monster from the id."

With apologies to John Keats and his famous poem *Ode on a Grecian Urn*, we humans have turned resentment into an art form, figuratively asking ourselves, "What can make me resentful? Let me count the ways." We can be resentful and seek revenge when people harm us personally, when they harm other people we care about, and even when they make bad choices and harm themselves. We can invent reasons for resentment and then use our resentment as an excuse to hide. We can even resent ourselves, allowing our mistakes to diminish our sense of self-worth. When we resent ourselves we may take revenge by telling ourselves that we are defective and that we don't matter. Some of us go even further and turn to drugs and/or alcohol to hide from our feelings of inadequacy, guilt and shame.

For addicts in recovery, resentment and revenge can also be a means of "switching addictions." Instead of stimulating ourselves with illegal drugs, alcohol, food or gambling, we may experience a "high" by obsessing over the harms that others have done to us and plotting revenge. But just like other stimulants that seem initially to produce attractive consequences, *resentment is ultimately self-destructive.* As a slogan in Twelve Step programs teaches me, "Holding on to resentment is like swallowing poison and expecting another person to die." The slogan reminds me that while we may resent and seek to take revenge against others, *resentment ultimately harms the people who hold on to it.* When our actions reflect resentment and revenge, we are reacting to people's mistakes rather than to their humanity and in so doing we diminish our own humanity. When we hold on to even justifiable resentments, we allow negativity to overpower our impulse to act righteously. This second commitment reminds me that I need to diminish resentment *for my own sake, and not only for the sake of the people I resent.*

FORGIVENESS

As imperfect humans, we may never rid ourselves entirely of resentment and the desire to take revenge. But we can diminish the power of resentment over our actions by *practicing forgiveness*. As with resentment, we reflect forgiveness through our actions and not our statements, feelings or intentions. As my friend Reverend Mark Whitlock taught me, we practice forgiveness when we substitute spiritual *F-You* (*Forgive* You) actions for revengeful *F-U!* (the *other* F.U.) actions. We practice forgiveness when instead of taking revenge *against* the targets of our resentment, we act righteously *towards* them.

When we refuse to wallow in resentment and instead practice forgiveness, we diminish resentment's power to control our actions. Acts of forgiveness leave the brokenness of the past in the past so that we can better restore wholeness to the future. Forgiveness allows us to extend bridges rather than raise walls. Forgiveness reminds us to be tolerant of the mistakes of others, just as we hope and expect that others will be tolerant of our mistakes. Forgiveness ultimately builds community because when our actions demonstrate compassion, understanding and openness we don't have to hide from each other.

Forgiving is not forgetting. I forgive in order to diminish the grip of negative past events on my present and future actions and relationships. But forgiveness does not require me to blind myself to the events that gave rise to resentment. For example, I can forgive a person who borrowed my car and damaged it, but I don't have to lend my car to that person again. Forgiving people while protecting myself against future harm allows me to avoid the destructive power of resentment and protect important relationships.

MOVING FROM F-U! (RESENTMENT) TOWARDS F-YOU (FORGIVE YOU).

You may say, "Okay Rabbi, I accept that resentment can undermine my quality of life. I'd like to be more forgiving. But my resentments are well founded. I am resentful only of people who have hurt or disappointed me. I'd love to wave a magic wand and free myself of many of my resentments, but I don't have one. What do you suggest?"

I'll begin my response with a confession: I don't have a magic wand either. My goal in fulfilling this commitment is to try each day to be at least a grain of sand more forgiving than I was the day before. Here are tools that help me take actions that reduce the power of resentment to control my actions so I can move in the direction of forgiveness.

SEE BEYOND THE LEOPARD

One spiritual practice that helps me to practice forgiveness is to recognize the possibility of changed behavior. Too many of us are prone to blindly accepting the Biblical teaching, "A leopard doesn't change its spots." (Jeremiah 13:23) *But we overlook the second half of this teaching!* The full Biblical teaching is, "A leopard doesn't change its spots, also you are able to do good even though you have learned evil." The second half of the verse teaches me never to write myself or others off. No matter what our past mistakes, we can change and we can do better going forward. We practice forgiveness and see beyond the leopard when we are honest with people about how they have harmed or hurt us and when we give them a chance to demonstrate their willingness to do better.

We also see beyond the leopard when we stay in the present so that we can see what is right in front of us. We can do this by asking ourselves, "Am I telling myself the truth about a person's present behavior or am I judging the person according to past actions?" We should not blind ourselves to a person's past misdeeds. But we can respect other people's dignity and accord them the benefit of the doubt when our reactions to present behavior are not controlled by our resentment of past behavior.

SEE MY PART

Another spiritual practice that helps me to diminish resentment and practice forgiveness is to ask myself, "What was my part in the events leading to my resentment?" Even when I am "justifiably resentful," the question often leads me to understand that my own actions are at least partly responsible for my resentment. For example, I have often been resentful of drivers whose slow pace and indecision has made me late for an appointment. But when I think about my part in the events, I often have to acknowledge that I didn't leave early enough for the appointment. Understanding my own part in the late arrival diminishes my resentment of the other driver.

On a much larger scale, the resentment of hundreds of people was fueled by their unwillingness to understand their part in the Bernard Madoff financial fiasco. Some years ago, investors handed over millions of dollars to Madoff, a supposed investment guru. Madoff attracted these investors by promising them guaranteed returns that were much higher than they could earn anywhere else. Many of the investors lost huge sums of money when it turned out that Madoff was running an illegal Ponzi scheme, paying off earlier investors not with legitimate profits but with money he raised from later investors. Madoff went to prison, but many investors were left with little more than anger and resentment towards Madoff for stealing their money. Without excusing Madoff, I suspect that few of loudest complainers were willing to examine their part in the events. Their part consisted of greed and the desire to get something for nothing that led them to believe Madoff's promises of guaranteed huge profits.

My part in events giving rise to resentment may also consist of my unrealistic expectations of another person. For instance, I may resent a Beit T'Shuvah employee who violated the trust I had placed in her. But when I think about my part, I may come to understand that I had unrealistic expectations about the employee's readiness for carrying out the responsibilities I had given her. As Twelve Step wisdom teaches me, "Expectations are resentments waiting to happen."

LOSE THE LABEL

Another forgiveness tool for diminishing resentment is to *lose the label and see the person*. Resentment can lead me to label people as liars, cheats or phonies. I am better able to practice forgiveness when I eschew the label and see the person. I see the person when, as Father Greg Boyle taught me, I ask myself, "Can I erase the margins between us and see aspects of myself in the other person?" I see the person when I ask, "Did she or he do the best they could at the time?" And I see the person when I recognize that actions are often the result of circumstances rather than a reflection of character. We practice forgiveness when we recognize that a person who has told a lie is not therefore a liar.

DON'T WAIT FOR THE AMENDS

For many years, one of my practices was not to forgive a person who had hurt or disappointed me until after the person had made amends to me. As my ninth commitment (see Chapter Eleven) makes clear, true amends includes much more than saying something like, "Sorry, let's move on." But I was unable to forgive people until they had at least told me that they regretted doing wrong.

I no longer insist on amends in any form as a condition of forgiveness because *I practice forgiveness for my own sake and not only for the sake of the people I forgive.* When I practice forgiveness despite the lack of amends, perhaps the person I forgive will at some point make amends to me. But as the Serenity Prayer teaches me, I must "accept the things I cannot change." I cannot change the actions of other people, nevertheless I can practice forgiveness for my own sake.

SET A DATE

Calendars provide opportunities for working on diminishing our resentments. For example, some of us make New Year's Resolutions on January 1. For Jews, Yom Kippur is a day for taking responsibility for our lives and committing to not letting old traumas hide our light and our soul and prevent us from living well. For Catholics there is Lent and for Muslims there is Ramadan. Whether we are religious or secular, the calendar can be our friend, usually providing a specific period of time to examine our resentments and think about how we can go about diminishing them by practicing forgiveness. We may not always carry out our resolutions and commitments, but whatever we leave unfinished today we can try to do better tomorrow.

A TORAH DRASH 1

A Forgiving God

The *paraha Va-yakhel* translates to "and he convoked." After the episode of the Golden Calf, Moses has gathered the Israelites and passed along God's message that despite the grievous mistake of the Golden Calf, they have the opportunity to move forward in their lives. WOW!! In this Torah portion, God validates the idea that change is possible, that repentance is real, and that forgiveness is a necessary action to take if we are to live well.

As we see all too often, people are quick to anger and to stay angry. One mistake can wipe out the memory of a person's good deeds. In my work as a rabbi, I have made mistakes and, to the best of my ability, have made *t'shuvah*. While I still have work to do, I have also done very well and continue to move forward in both of these areas of my life: what I do well and what I need to improve upon. Yet, people get angry and resentful. I am told, "All you care about is money," by people who have paid nothing for their treatment and are doing well in their lives. This burden that I put on some people makes me a "bad guy" and then all the good that I— and Beit T'Shuvah—have done for them, is forgotten.

This Torah portion teaches us to practice forgiveness. God forgave our ancestors of the worst sin: idolatry. God continues to forgive our practicing idolatry in all the forms we find today. People change all the time. I don't want to be seen as only the con man, thief, and drunk that I was at one time. I want to be seen for who I was then and am now. I know that there are people who want to live in the past and not see what is different today. I know that there are people who don't believe or accept anyone's *t'shuvah* or apology. I know that there are people who are fuelled by resentment and think forgiveness is for "sissies," "lightweights," or "those people." This Torah portion reminds us to practice *F-You*. Then we can relieve much of the stress, anger, and wasted energy that keeps us rooted in the anger of the past and replace it with gratitude and compassion.

A TORAH DRASH 2

The Foreskin of Our Hearts

In the *parsha Eikev*, Moses rails against the Israelites for their transgressions. Moses is hurt, and he believes that the people and God betrayed him by denying him entry into the Promised Land. I understand his anger. I have lashed out often at people who I think have hurt or betrayed me. But when I lash out in anger at others I victimize myself by detracting from my spirit. To diminish my hurt and anger I have to practice forgiveness, and in this *parsha* Moses teaches us how to do it: we have to circumcise the foreskin of our hearts. When we rid ourselves of the barrier to our heart, we can open our heart to others. This is not a one-and-done thing. The lesson of this *parsha* and of the Twelve Step programs is that we have to renew our commitment to forgive each day. Each day I have to remember that the hurtful actions of others that I see as directed at me are usually the result of people just trying to take care of themselves and not thinking about me. I am often guilty of this kind of behavior too. When I heed Moses' advice and each day commit to circumcising the foreskin of my heart, I live with hope and anticipation for the future rather than in resentment of the past.

SHARES FROM THE SHUV: PRACTICING FORGIVENESS

A Matter of Death and Life
Lance W.

I have celebrated more than twenty years of sobriety at Beit T'Shuvah Friday night services. I had been paroled to Beit T'Shuvah after serving about twenty years of a life sentence in a California prison for killing a young man during a drug-induced rage. I was loaded during the first few years of imprisonment; most people who have never been to prison have no idea how easy it is for inmates to buy and sell drugs.

I know my exact sobriety date—not only the date but also the time: 1:30 AM on a March 11, over twenty-five years ago. At that moment I was writhing in agony on the floor of my prison cell, too sick from the drugs I had taken even to stand up. For reasons I will probably never understand, that was my moment of clarity. I had been raised as a faithful Lutheran, and as sick as I was in that prison cell, I raised myself to my knees and prayed to God for the strength to stop using drugs. From that moment on, with the help of prison Alcoholics Anonymous meetings, I have stayed sober.

I experienced a spiritual crisis after I had been sober for about seven years. I questioned my commitment to sobriety. Here I was, a lifer who had taken another person's life and was unlikely ever to be paroled. If I was going to be confined in prison, what did it matter whether I was loaded or sober?

Amazingly, I was in the midst of my spiritual crisis when I heard about Beit T'Shuvah. I wrote a letter to Rabbi Mark, saying that even though I probably had no chance of leaving prison, I was desperate to stay sober because I thought I could still be of service to other prisoners who had a chance for release. That started years of correspondence between the two of us, in which we discussed how the teachings of our different religious traditions could help us live better. Rabbi Mark also visited me in prison a couple of times; no one else did.

As I approached eighteen years of sobriety, all in prison, I appeared at a parole hearing that changed my life. My victim's mother came to that hearing, looked at me, and testified through her tears that although she missed her son at every moment of her life, as a Christian she was ready and willing to forgive me. Based on her testimony, my regular attendance at A.A. meetings and my service to other inmates and the prison, I was paroled to Beit T'Shuvah. Ever since that parole hearing, every time I take a sober birthday cake I thank the mother for her testimony and dedicate my cake to her son. I can never return him to life, but I can honor his life and his memory by being the best version of myself that I can be. I worked as a spiritual counselor at Beit T'Shuvah, doing my best to help other addicts learn how to live decently, and now I am in private practice as a drug and alcohol counselor. I speak to groups at schools and community centers as often as I can.

Let Down by the Experts
Kathy H.

My husband and I are the parents of "Matt," who is twenty years old. By the time he was six years old, we had already sought help for Matt because he was doing poorly in school. We took Matt to one expert after another: educational therapists, psychologists, you name it. They each led us to believe that they could help Matt, but none of them was successful.

Over the years, the endless parade of professionals only seemed to cause our son more sadness and frustration. Nor did any of them figure out that he had become a frequent drug user. Through one fruitless effort to help Matt after another, my husband and I argued with each other and we were furious with all the so-called experts. Our marriage was in trouble by the time Matt overdosed when he was seventeen and a half years old. He might have died, but after detoxing, he agreed to long-term sober living and my husband and I started attending a parents-focused Al-Anon meeting.

I started to work the Twelve Steps. As part of my fourth step inventory, I wrote down the names of the nine experts whom I resented with every fiber of my being for giving us the false hope that they could help our son. I resented the countless hours and thousands of dollars wasted on these so-called professionals. I stared angrily at their names every day and I recorded my feelings about them in a journal. I wrote about how much my resentment of the experts was negatively affecting my relationships. I realized that my resentments were leading me to be increasingly angry and argumentative with Matt, with my husband and other family members and even with our friends. My resentment of the experts allowed them to continue to control my life.

I was desperate to put the past in the past, so I began to focus my journaling more and more on what I could do to forgive them. One day at a time, I began to see them as flawed human beings who probably did their best to help Matt. My resentments slowly dissipated, and my journal entries became less angry. Now when I look at that list of nine professionals, I feel no resentment whatsoever. Those negative experiences no longer hold any power over me. I am once again grateful for my life.

My husband is a headmaster of an excellent private high school. Virtually all of the students go on to college, many of them to the country's most elite universities. In a recent email to my husband, the school's external affairs director asked which university Matt would be attending after graduation. A few months ago this presumptuous inquiry would have rekindled all of my resentments toward the experts: their failure had put us in the humiliating position of having to reveal that Matt, the son of the headmaster, would not be attending a four-year college, at least not now. But we felt no anger. Practicing forgiveness helped restore my husband and me to sanity and wholeness.

A Second Chance
Paul B.

When I was a college student, I found out that the director of a summer camp had secretly given me a second chance. After my freshman year I served as a volunteer counselor at the college's summer camp for low-income diabetic children. I enjoyed being a counselor, and so volunteered to return to the camp after my sophomore year. Not until it was nearly time for the camp program to begin did the camp director contact me and ask me to return as a counselor.

At the end of that second summer session, the camp director called me into his office. He told me that he had been reluctant to bring me back as a counselor. The previous summer, I had screwed up by focusing on the campers' illness and ordering them about instead of talking to campers about what interested them. He asked me to return only after another counselor had backed out at the last minute. He told me that he had called me into his office to tell me how happy he was that I had proved him wrong. I had changed from the first summer to the second. I had treated the children with dignity and respect and had participated in camp activities with them.

I am not sure what accounted for my changed behavior from one summer to the next. I do know that the director's words humbled me. Without my knowing, I had been the beneficiary of a second chance. Ever since that conversation in the camp director's office, I do my best to practice forgiveness by giving people the benefit of the doubt and affording them second chances.

CHAPTER FIVE

THIRD COMMITMENT

I will pursue righteous actions by wrestling with my conflicting desires to act selfishly and selflessly.

THE BIBLE'S THIRD Commandment states, "You shall not misuse the name of the Lord your God." We might misuse God's name by engaging in blasphemy or holding malicious beliefs or intentions. But in my understanding the greatest misuse of God's name is neglecting to do our best to heed the call of our impulse to act righteously. The principle that we fulfill our role as God's representatives on earth when we *act* righteously is embedded in the First Commandment, which links God's supremacy to God's acting to deliver the Israelites from bondage in Egypt.

My corollary third spiritual commitment is to reflect my understanding of my higher power in daily life by doing my best to act righteously. Discerning the next right action can be difficult; I may not always know which action is the right one for me to take. But I act righteously when I pursue the next right action through a process that I call *spiritual wrestling*. This process helps me act in a way that balances my legitimate needs and desires with those of the people who my actions are likely to affect.

ONE ACTION AT A TIME

Twelve Step programs teach us to live one day at a time. This principle is important to alcoholics and drug addicts who like me are intimidated by the thought of a lifetime of changed behavior. Indeed, for many people, addicts or not, a commitment to maintain any standard of changed behavior for a lifetime is intimidating, whether the change involves giving up cigarettes or chocolate or requires walking 10,000 steps a day. A commitment to living a day at a time breaks a lifetime of behavior into a daily series of behavioral chunks that are more manageable for most of us who seek to improve the quality of our lives.

When I focus on the next right action, I break down a single day into even more manageable chunks. My concern is what is in front of me in the moment. Regardless of my past successes and mistakes, and notwithstanding what might happen in the future, I ask myself, "At this moment and in this concrete situation, what action is the right one for me to take?"

THE TWO YETZERS

Righteous actions often do not appear neatly packaged and tied up with a bow. Doing my best to act righteously often involves harmonizing the demands of the conflicting desires that Jewish tradition refers to as the *yetzer hatov* and the *yetzer hara*. I understand the *yetzer hatov* as a selfless desire to care about and promote the welfare of people other than ourselves, whether they are family members, friends, community groups or the world as a whole. I understand the *yetzer hara* as a selfish desire to get our own way, to satisfy our private needs and interests. I reflect my selfish *yetzer hara* when I ask myself the inward-facing question, "What am I getting out of life?" And I reflect my *yetzer hatov* when I ask myself the outward-focused question, "What is life getting out of me?"

These conflicting desires in and of themselves are neither good nor bad. My commitment to pursue the next right action does *not* mean that I have to do all that I can to obey the selfless desire of my *yetzer hatov* while squelching the selfish voice of my *yetzer hara*. If I were to ignore my selfish desire to satisfy my own needs and interests, I would not matter to myself. And if I were to ignore my selfless desire to act in a way that demonstrates care and concern for others, I would not matter to anyone *but* myself. To matter to myself *and* to others, I have to acknowledge and engage with both of these desires in a process that I call *spiritual wrestling*.

SPIRITUAL WRESTLING

Spiritual wrestling is a process of doing my best to act righteously by harmonizing my conflicting desires so that I can *satisfy* **and** *transcend* my own needs and desires. Ideally each significant action I take will satisfy and transcend my needs and interests *in proper measure*, meaning that my actions reasonably balance my needs and interests with those of the people who my actions affect. Of course I will never do this perfectly. Sometimes my actions will overemphasize my own needs and interests, while at other times I may shortchange my own interests in order to please other people. But by doing my best each day to reflect my conflicting desires in my actions in proper measure, I respond to the wisdom of the great first century Jewish sage, Rabbi Hillel:

If I am not for myself, who will be for me?
If I am only for myself, what am I?
And if not now, when?

Rabbi Hillel's words teach me that a commitment to wrestle with my conflicting desires in the pursuit of the next right action helps me to take *both/and* rather than *either/or* actions. When I do my best to act in a way that recognizes and transcends my legitimate needs and interests, I matter to myself *and* I matter to others. I sometimes have to make amends to people whose legitimate needs I unfairly slight. I sometimes have to make amends to myself for not sufficiently taking care of my own needs. The commitment is to wrestle, not to always get it right. As long as I am willing to wrestle with my conflicting desires in the pursuit of the next right action, I do my best to serve as a representative of God's righteousness on earth.

One of the Bible's most well-known stories exemplifies the process of wrestling with conflicting desires in an effort to act righteously. In this story, Moses is tending to his sheep in the wilderness when he sees a burning bush. Moses is startled by the fire's failure to consume the bush. The story tells us that having captured Moses' attention with the burning bush, God tells him, in substance, that the Egyptians' enslavement of the Israelites is causing his people great suffering. God appoints Moses to head back to Egypt, tell Pharaoh to let the Israelites go, and lead them out of the land of bondage to freedom. Moses is doing well as a shepherd, and he is very reluctant to undertake this dangerous mission. But after repeated urgings by God, Moses heads on back to Egypt. You know the rest of the story.

In my understanding, the story describes the wrestling match that takes place in Moses' mind as he vacillates between the conflicting desires to act selfishly and selflessly. Moses' *yetzer hara* urges him to serve his own interests and stay in his wilderness home as a successful sheepherder. His *yetzer hatov* urges him to transcend his self-interest by returning to Egypt and trying to rescue his people from bondage. The degree of Moses' uncertainty is reflected in the length of the struggle. For Moses, reflecting these conflicting desires in his action in proper measure means a return to Egypt to lead his people out of slavery. While "proper measure" in this instance seemingly accords greater weight to Moses' selfless *yetzer hatov*, I also see his selfish *yetzer hara* at work in his desire to belong to a community of free people. I am certainly no Moses, but every day I can relate to his internal struggle to figure out how to act in accord with his inner spark of holiness by doing his best to reflect the conflicting desires of the *yetzer hatov* and the *yetzer hara* in proper measure.

ACTION-BASED QUESTIONS

According to the Talmud, a compilation of ancient rabbinic debates and wisdom, "We will have the answers to everything when the Messiah comes." Until that mythical event occurs, the "Q and A" process of spiritual wrestling is the best tool to use when trying to figure out the right answers for ourselves. I give myself the best chance to act righteously by asking myself questions that help me understand the important aspects of a situation. The traditions of Judaism (particularly the book of Leviticus) suggest questions that can lead to righteous actions; others emerge from my experiences and the circumstances in which I find myself. Of course your questions may be different from mine. While none of us can guarantee that our best thinking will always produce righteous actions, we act righteously when we are willing to ask ourselves questions such as these and answer them as honestly as we can.

Is it necessary for me to act now, or at all? If I act, am I doing for others what they are capable of doing for themselves? As I am reminded by the Twelve Step wisdom, "Don't just do something, sit there," is it necessary that I try to fix problems immediately or is "nothing" the next right action for me to take? Perhaps by doing nothing I can afford other people the chance to grow in wisdom even if I disagree with their actions.

Am I telling myself the truth about my motives? Is an action the result of my wanting to *do* good or wanting to *look* good? Is an action that I have told myself is in the best interest of Beit T'Shuvah as an institution really in my own best interest? Am I willing to overlook a resident's relapses because of the resident's financial resources regardless of the potential risk to the sobriety of other residents?

Am I fearful of taking the next right action? Am I reluctant to act because of the criticism that I might receive from other people? Am I afraid to act righteously because it will reveal that I did not act righteously in similar circumstances in the past?

Have I been willing to ask for help? Am I reluctant to ask for help from mentors or friends because I am afraid to look weak or indecisive? Am I willing to seek input from people whose viewpoints might disagree with mine?

Have I considered leaving my comfort zone and taking "contrary action"? Twelve Step wisdom teaches me, "Insanity consists of doing the same thing over and over and expecting a different result." This teaching reminds me to ask myself whether an action I am considering reflects a knee-jerk reaction or whether I have wrestled with the unique circumstances that are in front of me in pursuit of an individualized response.

Am I putting a stumbling block before the blind? Am I acting in a way that takes unfair advantage of other people's disabilities or lack of knowledge? Am I requiring others to fulfill unfair conditions before I am willing to act? Have I undermined a relationship that I value by insisting on being in the right just for the sake of winning an argument? Am I judging others by standards that I am unwilling to apply to myself?

Am I keeping laborers' wages overnight? Would an action be fair to the people who work with me and for me? Have I properly measured my own economic interests and other people's rights to a fair living standard? Am I fulfilling my own work responsibilities?

Have I insulted the deaf? Does an action reflect realistic expectations of others and of myself? Am I treating a person as "less than" because of his or her physical, emotional or intellectual limitations? Am I speaking in a way that I can be understood, and am I listening in a way that I can understand others? When I am unsure am I willing to ask for clarification?

I am not a spiritual know-it-all. The title of "rabbi" does not confer on me an unerring instinct to determine or judge the righteousness of actions, whether my own or the actions of others. My commitment is to *pursue* the next right action, knowing that I will not always succeed. But I do my best to fulfill this third commitment through continued willingness to harmonize my conflicting desires by answering honestly questions such as these before acting.

A TORAH DRASH

Jacob the Wrestler

The *parsha Vayishlach* translates to "and he sent." In this portion, Jacob wrestles with a man, an angel, his conscience or whatever you want to call this "dark night of the soul" that the Torah describes. This Torah portion is so important to me because I have to wrestle each day in the pursuit of the next right action.

The story of Jacob is the story of each of us because it is messy. Our lives are messy! We would like to package our lives into a simple and pretty box. But Jacob's story represents our constant need to wrestle with our competing impulses to act selfishly and selflessly. Neither one is all good or all bad. This need to wrestle is not a moral flaw; it is how we are hard-wired. My life has been and continues to be one of struggling with my conflicting impulses. But Jacob's story reminds me that there is nothing wrong with me. We all have to find our path, and I have to confront myself constantly to ensure that I integrate all of my parts and that I am in acceptance of my path.

Rabbi Mark's App Store
Action-Centered Prayer

Prayer and meditation have been important tools in my pursuit of the next right action. Because the God of my understanding dwells within me as an inner spark of holiness, I do not pray *upwards* or *outwards* in the hope that a divine force will tell me what to do or other human beings will do the right thing. Rather I pray *inwards*. The Jewish word for prayer, *l'hapitel,* translates as "to look inside oneself." Rabbi Abraham Joshua Heschel taught that prayer is an act of listening, and in fulfillment of this teaching I pray so that I can discern the call of my inner spark of holiness in order to identify the next right action for me to take. Prayer is a private space within which I wrestle with my conflicting impulses to act selflessly and selfishly. Inwards prayer centers on the only power or person whose actions I can affect: me.

My understanding of the Jewish tradition is that prayer is meaningless unless it is backed up by action. For example, my prayer for a friend's return to good health has no healing power. The prayer's power results from the action or actions with which I back it up. For instance, through prayer I can resolve to help out with chores or just sit at the friend's bedside, and in that way demonstrate to my friend that whether in sickness or in health, he or she continues to matter. And for my prayer for the well-being of the inhabitants of a community that has suffered a natural disaster to have meaning, I have to treat it as a promise to take an action that even if only in a small way contributes to the community's recovery.

The idea of prayer as a time to connect my conscious mind to my inner spark of holiness is echoed in a story in the Al-Anon book *Courage to Change*. The story tells of a wanderer in the woods who comes upon a child sitting on a rock. The child continuously recites the ABC's. The wanderer asks, "What are you doing?" and the child responds, "I'm saying my prayers." The wanderer replies, "I don't hear a prayer, only the letters of the alphabet." The child explains, "I don't know all the words, so I say the letters and God will know what I'm trying to say." The story teaches me that willingness to connect through prayer with my inner spark of holiness helps me to act righteously.

SHARES FROM THE SHUV: PURSUING RIGHT ACTIONS

F ... Your Feelings
Russell H.

I served twenty-seven years in a California prison for participating as the driver of a getaway car in a murder-for-hire plot while I was in the Marines. About a month into my parole I was alone, scared, virtually without means, and unsure of how to live outside prison walls. I had heard of Beit T'Shuvah while I was in prison. They took a chance on me and I am forever grateful. I eventually became part of the maintenance team and I met Lysa, the soulmate of my dreams who is an alumna of "the house." I can never restore the life that I helped to take away, but I can honor my victim's life through the daily pursuit of right actions, serving as a mentor to others who search for spiritual meaning, and reaching out to young people who are at risk of throwing away their lives as I did so much of mine. Rabbi Mark's teaching to take "right actions" no matter what I am feeling or going through helps me live decently, and with joy, gratitude, trust and love for every day I am free. My shorthand understanding of the teaching is that I have to "F... my feelings" and do what is right.

This teaching was behind an important decision I made recently. I had become the facilities director for Beit T'Shuvah, a position that was a huge challenge for me. The facilities had to pass an important inspection that was to be conducted by a national accreditation group, and I did not want to fail the organization that had put so much into me.

About one month prior to the scheduled survey date, a resident of Beit T'Shuvah asked me to add him to my team as an intern in the maintenance department. The resident had absolutely no prior experience in maintenance, so I asked him why he thought I should take him on. He told me that he needed to do everything differently than he previously had, because the way he had been living his life to that point was not working. I was in turmoil. With the pressure of the upcoming inspection causing me so much anxiety, I did not want to be stuck with an inexperienced intern. But despite my fear and anxiety, I took the next right action: part of the maintenance department's mission is to train residents for responsible jobs, so I took on the resident as a new intern. We passed the inspection with flying colors, and almost equally gratifying is that the resident I took a chance on is now training another maintenance department intern.

A New Life
Kevin S-B

I had been addicted to methamphetamine for about a decade before I entered Beit T'Shuvah. I was living in a motel when I was arrested for possession of meth, and since this was my first offense the judge allowed me to go to rehab as an alternative to doing jail time. I had wanted to get off meth for months before my arrest, but I just didn't know how to change my life. Though my teeth were rotten and my body was wasting away, I had lived for so long as a meth addict that I didn't know how to live any differently.

Being arrested was the best thing that ever happened to me because it resulted in my being willing to accept help. The most important principle I learned at Beit T'Shuvah is to take the next right action. I'm sure it saved my life. When I was using the thought of changing my whole life overwhelmed me. My recovery really started when I realized that I could take life one action at a time. I learned to stay in the present, to see what was right in front of me and take what I thought was the next right action. No matter what I felt like doing, all that mattered was what I did. One action at a time (not all of them right, I didn't have to be perfect), I became a human being at Beit T'Shuvah.

I was a lost soul when I went into Beit T'Shuvah. I had given up on myself and I thought that my family and friends had given up on me too. When I moved out of Beit T'Shuvah, it's not that I got my life back: I had gotten a life.

Oh, Brother!
Rabbi Mark

During the years that I was stealing and abusing drugs and alcohol, my brother Neal led a good life and became a respected rabbi. Neal almost always came through for me on the many occasions that I begged him to loan me money, usually by lying to him that I was in the process of turning my life around and just needed a little help to get rid of the wreckage of my past.

Neal wasn't so gullible that he believed my lies. But at the time he believed that giving me money was the right action for him to take because his motive was to demonstrate his love and concern for me. As he reconsidered his actions in later years, Neal came to understand that his actual motive was self-interest. Sending me money allowed him to avoid the consequences of having to confront my disease and me. As long as I had enough money to get by, I would not show up at his door and he would not be burdened by trying to figure out what to do with me. Identifying his real motive in later years has helped Neal think about what the right action is for him to take when someone asks for help.

Silent Service
A Friend

Beit T'Shuvah was our son's third rehab. Over the years that he had struggled with addiction, my wife and I had attended many Al-Anon and other group meetings. The first Sunday that our son was in Beit T'Shuvah, he called and said that he was waiting for us to stop by for a visit. However, that afternoon we were at a friend's birthday party, and later that evening we had tickets for a show. Our son was furious, screaming at us that we didn't love him and had abandoned him. He said that he didn't care if he never saw us again and terminated the conversation. My wife and I were very upset, and we wanted to fix things immediately by calling back and assuring our son of our continuing love and hopes for him. Nevertheless, in accord with the Twelve Step slogan, "Don't just do something, sit there," we decided that the next right action for us to take was to do nothing. We did not call back or change our plans; instead we enjoyed the birthday party and the show. Our son did call us the next day to tell us about the interesting group meeting he had attended earlier that morning. The anger and resentment of the day before had vanished without our lifting a finger.

We understood that recovery is typically filled with ups and downs. We do not benefit our son by congratulating him for every peak and trying to rescue him from every valley. The Twelve Step slogan that reminds us that the next right action may be to do nothing is an important part of our recovery from our obsession with our son's addiction.

CHAPTER SIX

FOURTH COMMITMENT

I will assess my actions regularly with spiritual inventories.

THE BIBLE'S FOURTH Commandment reads, "Remember the Sabbath Day and keep it holy. Six days shall you do labor and work, but the seventh day is a day of rest unto Adonai, your God. You shall not do any work. You, your son, your daughter, your male, your female slave, your cattle or the stranger who is within your settlement." In my understanding the commandment creates a weekly opportunity for active spiritual renewal rather than a weekly chance to be a couch potato.

My corollary fourth spiritual commitment is to prepare regular spiritual inventories. Regular *spiritual time-outs* give me a chance to assess my recent actions and identify the righteous acts that I am proud of and the instances in which my acts have missed the mark. The process of preparing formal or informal personal inventories helps me to build on what I have done well and to think about how to avoid repeating my mistakes, while also making amends for them when appropriate.

SLOWING THE PACE

With the exception of my rabid (and in most years frustrating) passion for Cleveland's professional sports teams, I am not a sports nut. Yet I am familiar enough with sports to know that successful athletes often make comments along the lines of, "When I am playing well, the game slows down for me." When athletes say that a game slows down, I understand them to mean that they have been able to use their experience to recognize situations that tend to recur as games unfold and to develop plans for responding to them. These plans in turn make it more likely that they will respond effectively when those situations arise in the course of a game.

Just as athletes play better when they slow down the pace of a game, I improve my ability to act righteously when I use spiritual time-outs to slow down the pace of life. Spiritual time-outs are the spaces in which I can reflect on my actions, both those that I feel good about and those that I regret. These spaces give me the opportunity to connect my actions to the inner thinking and external circumstances that led to them. Recognizing my patterns of reactions to circumstances that are likely to recur in my personal and professional life helps me develop plans that make it more likely that I will take the next right action in the future.

SPIRITUAL INVENTORIES

A spiritual inventory is an *accounting of the soul* in which I acknowledge the character traits and actions that I feel good about and those that are bothering me. An inventory is a tool for renewing my commitment to living a richer and more meaningful life. Spiritual inventories provide me with the space to answer as honestly as I can questions such as:

> How have my recent actions reflected my positive character traits?
> What have I done to work on my character flaws and minimize their influence on my actions?
> How well have I balanced my conflicting desires to be selfish and selfless in the daily pursuit of righteous actions?
> What was it about my thinking or surrounding circumstances that led me to act righteously or to make mistakes?

When I address questions such as these I take my *spiritual temperature*. I find out what actions are prominent in my mind and at that moment how well these actions fulfill my commitments to live decently with daily purpose and to make my small corner of the world a place of compassion and justice.

Step Four of the Alcoholics Anonymous Twelve Step program calls upon participants to make "searching and fearless moral inventories" of their lives. The time commitment and level of detail suggested by the language of Step Four can be intimidating. But in my experience a spiritual inventory, even if it consists of a short end-of-the-day mental review of my actions, can help me to take my spiritual temperature. Alternatively an inventory may be longer and more formally recorded as an electronic document, and perhaps prepared with the help of a spiritual partner such as a sponsor, mentor or friend. What is important for me is to prepare inventories regularly at whatever level of formality and detail suits my present need to stay connected to my inner spark of holiness through truthful, timely and regular accountings of my significant actions.

To give you a more concrete sense of what an inventory might consist of when you have the time to prepare a formalized one, my inventories typically include the following three sections:

Character Traits

This section identifies character strengths and defects as they were reflected in recent actions either that I am proud of or that I regard as mistakes.

For example, for many years one of the character defects that I identified in inventories was my need to please other people and live up to their expectations of me. This defect nearly prevented me from trying to become a rabbi, because I believed that I would never be as learned in Torah and Jewish literature as people expected a rabbi to be. In recent years I have been able to include "self-esteem" as a positive character trait, because I am content to live my purpose and do my best to become the best version of Mark Borovitz that I can be regardless of whether I live up to other peoples' expectations of me.

Impatience has regularly appeared in my inventories as a character defect. I want people to act righteously according to my time schedule rather than theirs. Though I accept the Alcoholics Anonymous slogan, "you are ready when you are ready," my actions all too often display impatience with people who stay stuck in the same kind of thinking and behavior that diminishes their ability to live well.

Righteous Acts

I devote a second section of a spiritual inventory to righteous acts that I am proud of. You might think that including this section in an inventory is a no-brainer. But when I think back over recent actions I almost automatically focus on my mistakes and character flaws. I have to push myself to think about what I have done well because I tend to take my good deeds for granted. I often tell myself that I did only what I was supposed to do, or that anyone would have done what I did, or that I don't like to seem like I'm bragging, even to myself. Rationalizations such as this are wrong, because identifying the righteous acts that make us proud helps us to continue to act righteously. So if I mention in an inventory that I listened empathically without giving advice to a friend who was in pain and just needed to talk, this helps me be an empathic listener in the future.

Questions that you may ask yourself when you prepare this portion of an inventory include:

> How did I reflect my commitments in my actions?
> How was I of service?
> How did I tend to my side of the street while allowing others to take care of their own?
> How did I use my unique gifts and talents to live a rich and meaningful life?

Actions that Missed the Mark.

The third section of an inventory consists of mistakes and misdeeds. This section helps me to think about whether I need to make amends and about how I might do better in the future.

For example, an item that used to pop up frequently in my inventories was my disrespectful habit of staring at my computer screen while I talked to people in my office. I apologized publicly for my destructive behavior to the entire Beit T'Shuvah congregation during a Friday night service, as well as privately to as many of the individuals that I had wronged as I could. Listing this bad habit in my inventories also led to me develop and follow through on a simple plan for changing my behavior: moving conversations to a desk without a computer screen.

Questions that you may ask yourself when preparing this section of an inventory include:

> Did I miss the mark by acting from excessive guilt and shame because of my past mistakes and misdeeds?

Did I miss the mark by engaging in self-pity and acting from a sense that I was worthless and that I didn't matter?

Did I miss the mark by acting in a way that betrayed the trust that was placed in me by others, or that I placed in myself?

Did I miss the mark by spending too much time or too little time on others or myself?

Did I miss the mark by speaking ill of other people, even if what I said was accurate?

Did I miss the mark by lying to myself about my motives for acting?

Did I miss the mark by trying to control the actions of other people?

Did I miss the mark because I acted from fear or because I was too fearful to act?

SPIRITUAL GUIDES

The famous nineteenth century Scottish poet Robert Burns wrote the immortal lines:

"O wad some Power the giftie gie us,

To see oursels as ithers see us!"1

Burns' wisdom teaches me the value of seeking help from a trusted spiritual guide when preparing a spiritual inventory. Spiritual guides can help us see the whole picture, filling the gap created by our inability to see ourselves as others see us. They can help us see "the other side of the moon," the parts of the truth we often miss when we stay inside our own heads.

To honor my eighth commitment (see Chapter Ten) I nurture my soul with spiritual partnerships. And I may turn to one of my spiritual partners when I want help with a spiritual inventory. But a spiritual guide needn't be a spiritual partner. A helpful guide can be anyone whose advice you value and whom you trust to tell you their truth about who you are and what you have done.

A recent conversation with a Beit T'Shuvah congregant concerning spiritual inventories provided an excellent example of how a spiritual guide can help us understand "the whole truth." The congregant was the father of a high school-age son. He told me that he had recently prepared a spiritual inventory with the help of a spiritual guide who was a longtime friend. One of the actions they reviewed was the father telling his son that he didn't have to go to college to be successful. Learning issues had caused the son to struggle in school, so the father wanted his son to understand that with his wonderful artistic ability he didn't necessarily need to go to college; he could do very well in a career such as an interior designer or a set decorator. The guide responded by asking the father to think about how his son might have reacted to this advice. As they discussed the situation, the father realized that his son might well have interpreted his advice as meaning, "You're not smart enough to go to college." As a result, the father spoke to his son and apologized for the unintended slight. The son was grateful for his father's apology, and the episode strengthened the bond between them. The spiritual guide's quiet question helped this loving father to see a part of the truth that he couldn't see on his own.

SAMPLE INVENTORY ENTRIES

A bit of wisdom in the Talmud (a collection of rabbinic commentaries on the Torah) teaches that all beginnings are hard. This phrase certainly applied to my initial attitude towards spiritual inventories. Until I internalized the process of regularly using inventories to take my spiritual temperature, I was reluctant to devote sufficient attention to their preparation for inventories to have any meaningful impact on my actions. If you are new to the inventory process and beginnings tend to be difficult for you too, the following examples of inventory entries may be helpful. They are based on inventories prepared by various people and are by no means ideal specimens that you should try to emulate. Your inventories should reflect your experiences and your style. And if you are like me, the process of preparing an inventory will be more important than the specific words that you use. The examples below pair character traits with related actions, but I use this format simply for purposes of illustration.

- *Positive Character Trait 1*: "I can say what I honestly think even if I know the person I talk to won't agree with me. Not everybody has to like me or agree with me."
- *Positive Action 1*: "I volunteer to help set up the sound for the band that plays music during events hosted by a small non-profit group.

Just before one performance, a band member came to me and asked me to adjust the sound mix. I told him that at the last minute I did not have the time to do that; he should have asked me to check the mixer earlier. He was upset, but I refused to turn his problem into my problem. We continue to work together, I just know that I can't control what he does or how he reacts to the way I do my best to carry out my job."

- *Negative Character Trait 2*: "I'm a fixer. I grew up always trying to fix my parents' problems. Now I always try to fix my children and other people, and I feel responsible for their problems when I can't."

- *Negative Action 2*: "My daughter had waited until the last day to pay a parking ticket before the fine would go up a lot. She told me that she was too busy to show up at the traffic ticket clerk's office, and so she asked me to pay it for her. I cancelled my plans and waited in line for two hours to clean up her mess. I totally disregarded my own needs in favor of hers and I was so resentful."

- *Positive Character Trait 3*: "I stay out of my grown children's lives. I don't give advice unless they ask for it, not even in the form of rhetorical questions asking them if they've thought of all the possible downsides of their intended plans."

- *Positive Action 3*: "My son and his wife planned to purchase their first house. The house was very close to a busy road, and I was worried about things like noise and pollution. I would have expressed my concerns had they asked for my opinion, but they didn't so I kept my mouth shut."

- *Negative Character Trait 4*: "When my feelings are hurt I isolate myself and give people the silent treatment. I hold on to resentments instead of trying to solve problems."

- *Negative Action 4*: "My husband gave me a frying pan for Valentine's Day. It really upset me, especially because it was designed for low-fat cooking. Instead of telling him how the present made me feel, I didn't say anything for three days except "uh huh" or "uh uh" in response to his comments."

- *Positive Character Trait 5*: "Many relatives in my extended family were and are addicts. I married an addict and blamed all our problems on the addict. I've come to understand my part in our problems, and that a part of me that I had kept hidden from myself thrived on the drama and emotional swings of life with an addict. Exposing what

I kept hidden for so long is helping me to stop obsessing over my partner's choices."

- *Positive Action 5*: "When my partner was too drunk or hung over to attend family events, I used to stay away too, blaming illness or an emergency project at work. I no longer do that. In these situations I go alone if I want to be there. If I am asked to explain my partner's absence, I do not lie. I may tell them to check with my partner for an explanation."

- *Negative Character Trait 6*: "I am not comfortable reaching out to other people. I am alone too much, and I wait for my partner to come home from work and make me happy."

- *Negative Action 6*: "After our first child was born, I dropped out of my post-graduate program and suddenly was a stay-at-home mom. I love our child but I am very depressed. When my partner came home from work last week I got really angry because my partner just wanted to sit and watch television all night instead of paying attention to me."

- *Positive Character Trait 7*: "I am grateful for my many solid friendships. My friends support me when I am right, and they are willing to call me on my shit when I behave badly."

- *Positive Action 7*: "As a man, I never talked with my male friends unless I needed help or information. I have started getting together regularly for morning coffee and bagels with different friends, and I really look forward to our free-flowing and honest conversations."

- *Negative Character Trait 8*: "When things don't go as I want I wallow in self-pity. I compare myself to others, thinking that they are always luckier than I am and that my situation is so much worse than theirs."

- *Negative Action 8*: "I work for a large company in the shipping department. Another person in the department got a promotion that I thought I deserved more than she did. I congratulated her, but inside I was a mess, wondering why other people always get the goodies that ought to be mine."

Over the course of preparing inventories, you may discover (to your delight or dismay) that your perception of your character traits and actions may change over time. For example, I spoke not long ago with a congregant who over a series of personal inventories had identified "willingness to help others whenever needed" as a positive character trait. But as she continued to assess her character traits and actions, she moved this trait to the negative side of the ledger. She had come to understand that she had become a "people pleaser" or a "doormat" who was too willing to sacrifice her own needs and desires in an effort to satisfy other people. The revised understanding of her character led her to try to do better to balance her own needs and desires with those of others in proper measure.

A TORAH DRASH

Are We Good Enough?

The *parsha Shemini* tells the story of the entire Israelite community gathered together in front of their leaders, Moses, Aaron and Aaron's sons. Aaron is seized with uncertainty as to his fitness to become the High Priest of all the tribes, and Moses has to re-assure him that he is up to the job. I relate to Aaron's plight in the uncertainty I felt early on in my ability to be an effective rabbi and the spiritual leader of a treatment center that aimed to help addicts and alcoholics to reclaim their lives and live decently. Taking my spiritual temperature with the help of a more experienced rabbi and mentor, I described a recent troubling counseling session that I had had with a Beit T'Shuvah resident. I told him that I had been too impatient and quick to anger because of what I considered the resident's spotty behavior in early recovery. I confessed my worry that impatience and anger were character traits that were often likely to get in the way of my ability to be an effective spiritual counselor. My mentor helped me to understand that my fitness for my job was not based just on who I was now, but on my willingness to learn how to be better. This was a transformative moment for me. Like Jacob, I learned that owning up to my insecurities, fears and shame could serve as a pathway for growth and betterment.

Rabbi Mark's App Store
Spiritual "To Do" Lists

I think of a spiritual "to do" list as the portion of an inventory that I most want to focus on over a specific period of time—say, the next thirty days. For example, I might identify the character trait that I most want to build on, and the one type of mistake that I am most anxious to stop making. I used to keep spiritual to do lists on pieces of paper. Now I write and carry them around in my mobile phone. I have even installed a particularly significant to do list as electronic wallpaper.

Daily Action Inventories

On many days, I find it helpful to take a very informal daily spiritual inventory. I mentally review my activities, organizing them according to actions that I am proud of and actions that I am not so proud of. I reflect on both sets of actions, trying to understand how to make more of the former and less of the latter when opportunities arise. I know that I am not and never will be perfect, but conscious and fresh review of my actions promotes the likelihood that I can be a grain of sand better at taking right actions each day.

SHARES FROM THE SHUV: SPIRITUAL INVENTORIES

Role Play Inventories
A Friend

I am a professor at a large urban university. One of the courses that I frequently teach is a seminar in which students participate in out-of-class individual role-play exercises. An important part of these exercises is the de-briefing session that follows each role-play; that is when I can help students understand how to apply the principles we discuss in seminar meetings to the concrete scenario of a role-play.

I usually begin a de-briefing session by asking a student an open-ended question along the lines of, "How would you evaluate your performance?" Almost invariably, students concentrate on what they thought went badly. Most of their sentences start with "I should have said…" or "I never should have said…"

When I learned about spiritual inventories and began taking my own, I was struck by the similarity between my de-briefing sessions and my inventories. Though the contexts and settings are very different, de-briefing sessions and inventories are both opportunities to evaluate our actions. What struck me is that, just like my students, when I made spiritual inventories I almost always focused on my character defects and what I did badly. I am not nearly as good at recognizing my strengths and right actions. Just as I urge students during de-briefing sessions to think about what they did well, one of my tools for doing life better is to force myself to think about my character assets and what I have done well when I take spiritual inventories.

Topsy-Turvy
A Friend

My first serious effort at a spiritual inventory was a revelation. Many qualities and actions that I had always considered to be virtues and good deeds I came to understand as character defects and mistakes. By contrast, I had ignored many qualities and events that made me feel good about myself. I wasn't sufficiently involved in my own experiences to know what I did well and where I had missed the mark.

For example, I initially considered that one of my virtues was my willingness to sacrifice my financial security in order for our addicted daughter to go to a series of very expensive rehabs. I came to understand these actions as the result of a defect of character, because my willingness to sacrifice my own security was a measure of my lack of self-worth; I didn't think that I mattered enough to deserve to have a secure financial footing.

Before I started preparing spiritual inventories, I thought that there was something wrong with me because I was an introvert. I always resisted my parents' and teachers' advice that I should join groups and participate in activities. But when I began using inventories, I decided that there is nothing wrong with being an introvert. I have come to view this as one of my virtuous qualities. This is who I am for today. I can be a loving parent, a good friend and a happy person, all while remaining an introvert.

Better Late Than Never
A Friend

When my children were small, I stood by while my husband physically abused them. I overlooked his drinking and lied to my children and myself that if we were nicer to him the abuse would cease. When I began making spiritual inventories, I came to realize that my tolerance of my husband's horrible behavior was a character defect rather than a strength. Eventually I grew strong enough to kick my husband out of the house and get a divorce. I apologized to my children for having failed to protect them and arranged for therapy for them and for me. I used my inventories to keep myself strong by including "willingness to forgive myself for feeling too worthless to stop the abuse" as one of my character strengths. Now I am a different person who tries to empower other parents to take action against abusers by sharing my experiences and the value of personal inventories with them.

CHAPTER SEVEN

FIFTH COMMITMENT

I will honor my parents by acting from principle in all of my affairs.

THE BIBLE'S FIFTH Commandment states, "Honor your father and your mother, so that your days shall be long upon the land." As the commandment refers to "honor" rather than "love," I understand it to refer to the moral principles that connect one generation to another rather than to the emotional ties between parents and children. The commandment for me is a promise that when people act in accord with the moral principles of their ancestors, life on earth will continue until the end of days.

My corollary fifth spiritual commitment is to act from principle in all of my affairs. A central teaching of Alcoholics Anonymous and all Twelve Step programs is to place "principles above personalities." I carry out this teaching by doing my best to act from principle in all circumstances, regardless of my emotions or feelings. I seek to take the next right action whether my actions affect friends or strangers, the powerful or the powerless, and indeed even when my actions affect people who have wronged me.

DO IT ANYWAY

A commitment to act from principle in all of our affairs means doing our best to take the next right act action in all circumstances. Of course as a human being I am subject to a variety of feelings, emotions and attitudes. If I am angry with someone, this commitment is a reminder not to allow that anger to diminish my concern for that person's legitimate needs and interests.

Even affection for a friend can affect my willingness to act righteously, either by leading me to give short shrift to my own needs and desires or by protecting the friend from the consequences of their actions. At the end of the day we have to do the best we can to act righteously regardless of our statements, feelings, intentions or beliefs. My goal as always is to be a grain of sand better each day at acting from principle in all circumstances.

For example, when a person seeks my advice, my obligation is not to allow the person's status in the Beit T'Shuvah congregation or in the community at large to affect my response. If an action that I have taken has wronged another person, my willingness to make amends should not be affected by whether the person I wronged has at some other time wronged me or might at some future time be in a position to help me personally or donate to Beit T'Shuvah. As long as I can truthfully tell myself that I have done my best to act in accordance with my principles I matter to myself and others in a way that is uniquely mine.

The principle of separating actions from feelings is often one that parents and other loved ones of residents of Beit T'Shuvah have to learn. By the time addicts are willing to enter a treatment program and seek recovery, their loved ones have often spent years trying to "cure" them by supporting them, making excuses for their mistakes and cleaning up the damage resulting from their bad behavior. This commitment helps people in these situations to understand that feelings of love and concern can lead them to believe that they are helping addicts (and people who suffer from other maladies of the soul) to get better when in fact they are enabling them to continue using by shielding them from the negative consequences of their actions. Loved ones often have to recover along with addicts, learning how to put their feelings of love and affection to the side so that they can take the next right action.

My commitment to act fairly and with compassion in all of my affairs does not require me to blind myself to people's mistakes or misdeeds. But when I confront wrongdoers, whether they have broken the law or my trust, I can place principles above personalities by distinguishing people from their actions. For example, the right action may be for me to expel a resident from Beit T'Shuvah for failure to maintain sobriety. Yet I can still place principles above personalities through willingness to communicate my decision in a compassionate manner that distinguishes the resident from his or her actions. That is, I can truthfully describe the behavior that led me to expel the resident from the house and discuss my hope that the resident will learn from past mistakes and do better going forward. I can communicate my belief that whatever the resident's past mistakes, the resident's impulse to act righteously renews at each moment and awaits only their willingness to reflect that impulse in actions. While referring the resident to other recovery programs, I can also act from principle by discussing circumstance that might make it possible for them to seek re-admission to Beit T'Shuvah should they be interested in doing so.

A PEDESTAL OF EXPECTATIONS

As much as I can struggle to hold fast to this commitment when I interact with people who have acted badly, my struggle can be even greater when I put people on a "pedestal of expectations." That is, I may be so impressed by a person's background or talents that I neglect to distinguish people from their actions. As a result I may fail to do what is right because I act according to my unrealistic expectations rather than according to the person's actions. To practice my principles in all my affairs, I have to focus on people's actions rather than on my expectations even when my expectations are positive rather than negative.

For example, some years ago I was in awe of one past resident's musical talent. This resident wrote and performed many songs whose words and melodies beautifully captured prayers' spiritual meanings. I neglected to distinguish the resident from her actions and put her on a pedestal of expectations by regularly extolling her recovery and her talent in front of the congregation and asking her to perform each week at Friday night services. I overlooked the resident's negative attitudes towards many Beit T'Shuvah employees and other residents; they were not reflective of a person who had embraced sobriety and recovery. The resident endured a series of relapses that resulted in expulsion from the house. While I do not blame myself for these relapses, the resident's experiences taught me a lesson that I have had to learn more than once: when I place people on the pedestal of my expectations, I dishonor their inner spark of holiness. I have to accord people the dignity of pursuing sobriety according to their needs and level of readiness. If I am to fulfill a commitment to place principles above personalities, I need to put expectations to the side and tell myself the truth about my own and other people's actions, both positive and negative.

GODLY MOMENTS

Rabbi Abraham Joshua Heschel taught, "One of the goals of life is to experience commonplace deeds as spiritual adventures." Rabbi Heschel's uplifting words remind me that when I act from principle as I carry out even the most mundane events of daily life, I have numerous opportunities to experience Godly Moments that add to spiritual buoyancy. When I smile at a passerby, wave a signaling driver into my lane of traffic, or pay attention to a store clerk instead of to a personal electronic device, I create a Godly Moment that communicates to another person that we both matter and that we exist in kinship with each other.

The so-called *broken windows* policy of policing holds that if the police protect neighborhoods by responding fairly but vigorously to petty crimes such as vandalism and noise pollution, crimes that are more serious are less likely to occur. My *broken spirit* policy is similar: when we approach ordinary activities as opportunities for Godly Moments, perhaps the spiritual buoyancy we experience helps us to pursue spiritual meaning in our more important affairs.

A TORAH DRASH 1

Weeping for our Enemies

The book of Exodus includes the story of the Israelites' escape from bondage in Egypt. Yet over the centuries, when Jews mark the escape from bondage at Passover Seders, the custom is for each person at the table to spill a drop of liquid from a cup while reciting the ten plagues that God visited upon the Egyptians before Pharaoh released the Jews from bondage. The spilled liquid represents tears. While the Egyptians may have enslaved the Israelites, Jews nevertheless symbolically weep because of the suffering that the Egyptians had to endure. The important lesson that this custom teaches us is to act in accord with the principle that human suffering is sad, whether the people who suffer are friends, strangers or enemies. The Passover custom reminds us of our obligation to do the best we can to alleviate human suffering.

A TORAH DRASH 2

Hineini

The *parsha Va-yetzei* translates to "he went out." Jacob has fled his home to escape the anger of his brother Esau, whose birthright he has stolen. The *parsha* describes Jacob's loyalty to his mother Rebekah, to his uncle Laban and to Laban's daughter Rachel, Jacob's intended bride. All of these people deceive Jacob. Rebekah lies to Jacob that he was born before his twin brother Esau. Laban tricks Jacob into working for him for fourteen years by promising Jacob falsely that he can marry Rachel. Rachel participated in the deception by allowing Jacob to marry her sister Leah.

After many years, Jacob answers *Hineini*, "Here I am," in response to God's call to return to his father and his homeland. Jacob is finally able to act from principle instead of from misguided loyalty to the people who tricked him. And when Laban wrongly accuses Jacob of theft, Jacob continues to act from principle when despite Laban's previous trickery, Jacob tells Laban that he will punish the actual thieves if Laban can identify them. The *parsha* teaches us that when we are loyal to people, we can lose our integrity. When we are loyal to our principles we can be our authentic and decent selves.

Rabbi Mark's App Store
At-One-Ment

The concept of "atonement" signifies a need to right a past wrong. A spiritual tool that transforms the word into a spiritual reminder of my obligation to act from principle in all of my affairs is to separate the word into syllables and pronounce it as *At-One-Ment. At-One-Ment* is a mantra that helps me connect my conscious mind to my soul and recognize my kinship with all other people regardless of their status or situation. The term motivates me to pursue the goal of contributing if even in a very small way to a world in which people are a little bit more kind to and compassionate with each other.

Spiritual "Helper Verbs"

In English grammar, a helper verb is an auxiliary word that extends the meaning of a verb. For example, in the simple sentence, "I had walked," the word "had" is a helper verb as it indicates that an action (walking) took place in the past.

I sustain my obligation to act from principle in all my affairs through a variety of tools that are the spiritual equivalent of helper verbs. The tools serve as figurative "strings around my finger," reminding me that I am obliged to do the best I can to act from principle in all of my affairs. Among the strings that I regularly place around my fingers are these:

- **Kosher meat**. While I do not observe the full panoply of the complex kosher practices, I eat meat only if it is kosher. This action keeps me connected to my inner spark of holiness by reminding me of the principle that we should not thoughtlessly destroy life simply to satisfy personal desires.

- **Kaddish Partners.** "Saying Kaddish" is a regular part of worship services at Beit T'Shuvah (and at virtually all Jewish houses of worship). During Kaddish, congregants keep alive the memories of deceased loved ones by standing up and saying their names aloud. During Kaddish, I make sure that no one mentioning a loved one's name stands alone. This action is a spiritual reminder of the kinship among all human beings, because the death of any person is a loss to the community as well as to an individual.

- **Spiritual Reading.** While spiritual lessons can emerge from any of the creative arts, reading is my principal artistic string around the finger for sustaining my obligation to practice my principles in all my affairs. I draw spiritual sustenance from authors across a wide spectrum of professional, spiritual and religious backgrounds. My particular favorites are the sociologist Eric Fromm, Reverend Martin Luther King, my good friend Father Greg Boyle (founder of Homeboy Industries, which has helped hundreds of gang members return to decency), my mentor Rabbi Ed Feinstein, and of course, Rabbi Abraham Joshua Heschel. The wisdom of writers such as these reminds me that the need to wrestle with our conflicting impulses to act selflessly and selfishly in the pursuit of righteous actions is ongoing, and that my obligation is to matter by doing my best to contribute at least a grain of sand of purpose, compassion and justice to the world each day.

SHARES FROM THE SHUV: PRINCIPLES ABOVE PERSONALITIES

A Party to Redemption
Jon E.

I came to Beit T'Shuvah on my knees, after eighteen stints in other rehabs and detox facilities. Beit T'Shuvah for me was the last house on the block. I had worked for a while in the catering industry, so after I had been a resident for about six weeks I was among the residents who were hired to pass around appetizers at a party. I had no appropriate clothes of my own to wear, but luckily another resident loaned me a white shirt and a clip-on tie. We were all driven to the party in one of Beit T'Shuvah's notoriously unreliable "druggy buggy" vans.

As we walked up to the front door I was startled to realize that I recognized the house where the party was being held. It was the house of the parents of one of my best friends through my elementary and high school years. I had spent lots of time playing with my friend in that house, and I never thought I'd return to it as an addicted loser who was lucky to have a job for a night. It turned out that the party was my former best friend's wedding, and I knew many of the people who were there. As I stood frozen, my friend's father recognized me and noticed how uncomfortable I was. He kindly suggested that I work in the kitchen so I wouldn't have to embarrass myself in front of people who knew me before addiction took over my life. The father's offer marks the moment when I decided to live according to principle and not hide in the expediency of the moment. I thanked the father for his offer and told him that I was hired to serve appetizers and that is what I would do. The next right action for me to take was to carry out the tasks that the father had hired me to perform. During that party, I got totally into my assignment and passed the hell out of those appetizers. That party took place over a decade ago, but I always think back to it when I am tempted to act from expediency rather than principle.

Honoring Mom
A Friend

I am Irish-Catholic and though I am not an addict, when my life was in chaos I sought the advice of Rabbi Mark at the suggestion of a friend who is a former Beit T'Shuvah resident. My parents had gotten divorced when I was a ten-year-old girl living in New York. My mom was devastated, and I felt responsible for taking care of her. I went to college in California and remained on the West Coast after graduation. My mom was still in New York, and living in California was partly my way of building a life of my own.

I came to see Rabbi Mark at a time when my mom's incessant demands were making my life unmanageable. She repeatedly and often tearfully insisted that I had to move back to New York and take care of her. But I was happy living in California and I was not about to move back to New York just to please my mom even though I felt really bad for her. I had attended Catholic schools and I was quite familiar with the Fifth Commandment. I felt an obligation to honor my mom, but I was not about to ignore my own needs just to please her.

Rabbi Mark helped me to think about the Fifth Commandment's use of the word "honor" rather than "love." While I lived at home, my mom had always encouraged me to be strong, independent and self-sufficient. I loved my mom, but the best way for me to honor the principles she stood for was for me to remain in California. At the same time, I could demonstrate my love for my mom in other ways. We set up a schedule of phone calls and visits, and I contacted friends of hers and arranged for them to call on her at mutually convenient times. I was loyal to my love for my mom and to my obligation to uphold the principles she had instilled in me.

Principled Parenting
Helen & Jerry S.

Our beloved son Steven struggled with alcohol and illegal drugs from his early teens until he lost the struggle to a crystal meth overdose at the age of twenty-six. Though Steven lost his battle with drugs, we are confident that by taking principled actions, we gave him the best chance we could of finding a path to sobriety and respectability.

After numerous incarcerations in juvenile halls and jails, Steven became a resident of Beit T'Shuvah. He had stayed there for about four months when he was dismissed because he relapsed on alcohol. But our association with Beit T'Shuvah and Al-Anon taught us to act from principle rather than from emotion. We accepted that Steven could maintain sobriety and live honorably only when he was ready and willing to do so; nothing that we could say or do could make him ready or willing to change his life. Steven was adopted at birth and had all the love and opportunities our family could offer. Unfortunately, he was predisposed to alcoholism, drugs and anger issues from his birth family.

Continuing to act from principle after Beit T'Shuvah kicked Steven out, we did not allow him to move back into our house, nor did we support him financially. Steven stayed with friends, lived on the streets and was in and out of jails for using and for probation violations. With a number of arrest warrants outstanding, Steven left L.A. and "did a geographic." He traveled from one state to another on buses and trains, working often enough to earn enough money to buy alcohol and drugs and getting DUIs often enough to become familiar with many county jails. We were happy when Steven called us from jail, because we knew that he had a roof over his head, a bed and food to eat. Whenever Steven contacted us, we told him that we could not help him, that we were sorry for his difficulties and that we loved him and wished him well.

After close to a year on the road, Steven called to tell us that he was done and that he was ready to live up to his obligation to take the next right action. His plan was to return voluntarily to L.A., and get a bed at Beit T'Shuvah. He was accepted back into the program as a day patient but when a bed became available, Steven was told that he couldn't stay there until he took care of his outstanding warrants. He wanted sobriety more than anything and he found the courage to turn himself into the police and serve the required jail time. Because he turned himself in, his sentence was slashed in half. Fifty-six days later, he was released and on the same day, he got the bed that Beit T'Shuvah promised him. This time, he was in with both feet and he adhered to the program. We were thrilled. We had given Steven the dignity of making his own choices, and he had at last chosen life. Steven followed through on his plan with no help from us. Steven left "the house" on good terms and he and his lovely girlfriend moved into an apartment. We were never closer to Steven; he frequently thanked us for sticking to our principles and allowing him to make his own choices. Steven enrolled in a technical training school and did so well that he made the Dean's and President's List for earning straight A's for three consecutive semesters. He even earned his certification in welding. He started interviewing for part-time jobs, being honest with potential employers about his history and his commitment to change. But in the midst of all this happiness and success, he went out one more time and it killed him.

Acting from principle allowed us to live with joy and purpose whether Steven was using or not. Our lives were far from perfect, but our commitment to "accept the things we could not change" allowed us to focus on what made us happy: friends, family, blue merle dogs (Australian Shepherd and Border Collie) and pet turtles/tortoises. When we joined an Al-Anon group for parents of alcoholics and addicts, we often heard the slogan, "Wait for the miracle." We initially understood this slogan as meaning that if we practiced the principles of Al-Anon, our son would eventually embrace sobriety and live decently. Certainly many of the parents in the hundreds of parent Al-Anon meetings that we have attended have experienced that miracle. But despite our son's death, we too have experienced a miracle through our willingness to practice the spiritual principles of our program in all of our affairs. Our miracle is that we lived with purpose and joy while our son was alive, and that we have continued to live with purpose and joy since his death. Of course we are sad, and we feel his loss every day. But his life and his choices were his. Our principled actions allowed us to live our lives with serenity and Steven to decide to choose life.

We honor Steven's memory by continuing to pursue principled actions and to share our experience, strength and hope with others. In fact, Helen sponsors numerous sponsees from our parent Al-Anon groups. And both of us continue to be "surrogate parents" to many past and present residents at Beit T'Shuvah whose family ties have been strained by addiction. Our life has become one of giving back and being of service.

CHAPTER EIGHT

SIXTH COMMITMENT

I will not murder my soul; I will live by acting with daily purpose.

THE SIXTH COMMANDMENT states, "You shall not murder." The commandment teaches us that human life is sacred. Murder is morally wrong because it is the ultimate rejection of God's command to choose life.

My corollary sixth spiritual commitment is not to murder my soul. Rather I will strengthen my soul's impulse to act righteously by recognizing my uniqueness and acting with daily purpose. I will not denigrate who I am or what I can do by comparing myself to others. Rather one day and grain of sand at a time I will seek to become the best possible version of myself.

PHYSICAL AND SPIRITUAL MURDER

We cannot *physically* murder our souls. But we commit *spiritual* murder when we de-value our unique skills and interests, and so ignore our soul's impulse to act righteously. I committed spiritual murder for the two decades that I forgot that I am a holy soul and chose to abuse substances and perpetrate felonies. We murder our souls when we compare ourselves to others and hide from a purposeful life that reflects our skills and passions because we fear that we are not as smart or as capable as other people are. We commit spiritual murder when we act out scripts that others have written for us, even if those scriptwriters care for us. We commit spiritual murder when we are tourists in our own lives, indifferent to our talents and interests instead of demonstrating appreciation for our chance to be alive by acting on purpose. We commit spiritual murder when we tell ourselves that we are nothing special or that we are not good enough. To paraphrase the late and great UCLA basketball coach John Wooden, we murder our spirit whenever we allow the things we cannot do to prevent us from doing the things we can do.

Physical murder is permanent, but fortunately *spiritual* murder is not. No matter how we have lived in the past, our inner spark of holiness is a *spiritual pilot light*. When we are willing to wrestle with our conflicting desires to act selfishly and selflessly, our soul's impulse to act righteously is available 24/7 to help us live with greater purpose and passion. Through this sixth commitment, I choose life by embracing the unique talents and interests that are the gift of my soul so that I can live with daily purpose.

I AM UNIQUE; SO ARE YOU

Each of us is an individual creation, not a stamped-out product of a mint or a machine. Will Rogers, the famed early twentieth century American humorist, captured our uniqueness by joking, "All of us are ignorant, only on different subjects." Rogers' wit reminds me of an equal and opposite truth: all of us are smart, except on different subjects. One of the spiritual maladies that long prevented me from acting decently was comparing myself to others and always coming up short. I focused on the skills and talents that other people had that I lacked, forgetting that I had talents and skills that they lacked. A similar spiritual malady is to dismiss the value of our talents and interests, internalizing outside messages that they lack social significance or telling ourselves, "Anybody else could do what I do." This commitment teaches us not to be "comparison shoppers." When we act with a daily purpose that reflects our unique humanity, truly no one else exists to whom we can compare ourselves.

When we value our unique talents and interests and act with daily purpose, we matter because *all righteous purposes are important.* For today, your daily purpose may be to expand human knowledge of the universe, to help frame a new building as part of a construction crew, to organize a rainy-day activity for children, to recover from an illness, to help out a friend who is ill or infirm, or to work as a volunteer for a group that reflects your talents and interests. Your daily purpose may encompass one or a number of activities, and your daily purpose may change over time as your talents and passions change. None of these purposes is more valuable than the others. Each of us has dignity, and none of us has greater human value than anyone else. When we do our best to act righteously, each of us lives with daily purpose in a way that nobody else can. Each of us is the only person who can do what we do in the way that we do it. We have a seat at the table that is ours alone to occupy. The world needs each of us because each of us can act righteously in a way that no one else can.

Will Rogers' humorous phrase echoes the Jewish understanding of uniqueness. Rabbi Zusya of Hanipol taught, "In the next world, they will not ask me, 'Why were you not more like Moses?' They will ask me, 'Why were you not more like Zusya?'" The unique value of every life finds expression in the Jewish teaching that if a person saves a single soul, it is as though the person has saved an entire world; but that if a person destroys a single soul, it is as though the person has destroyed an entire world. Because each of us is unique, every one of us matters.

EMBRACING UNIQUENESS

Embracing our unique daily purpose is an action, not an intention or a feeling. This means that we embrace our daily purpose by using our unique talents and interests to act righteously. I embraced a unique daily purpose when I enrolled in rabbinical school. Even after many years of sobriety I was afraid to take this step because I was still a "comparison shopper." I compared myself to my mentor Rabbi Ed Feinstein and many other rabbis I have known, including my brother Neal. I told myself that I was unworthy of attending rabbinical school, because I knew that I would never achieve their depth of knowledge of the Torah, the Talmud and other Jewish texts. I was able to pursue a rabbinical degree only when I became willing to stop comparing myself to others and thought instead about what I could bring to the table as the rabbi of Beit T'Shuvah. I realized that I would act with unique daily purpose even if I weren't the best and most learned rabbi. If I did my best to become the best and most learned version of Rabbi Mark, I would be of service to myself and to Beit T'Shuvah. By combining my talents with my desire to help as many people as I could to experience spiritual recovery I would have a richer and more meaningful life

The spiritual principle to take life a day at a time keeps me grateful that I can act with daily purpose today, even if I may hope to move toward a different or greater purpose tomorrow. For example, you may recall that

Harriet Rossetto asked me to organize bric-a-brac that people had donated to Beit T'Shuvah into a small thrift shop shortly after my release from prison. Even that modest task provided me with spiritual buoyancy because I understood that at the time I was in the right place and doing what I needed to be doing though I hoped to move towards a different purpose that I could not then foresee. But while I worked in that thrift shop my daily purpose was as important to my spiritual recovery then as my serving as Beit T'Shuvah's rabbi and spiritual leader is to my continued recovery now. And when new residents enter Beit T'Shuvah, counselors may ask little more of them than to make their bed, show up for meals and meetings and do house chores. In her book *Sacred Housekeeping*, Harriet discusses how seemingly menial tasks such as these promote spiritual recovery by providing residents with daily purpose while they work towards understanding and valuing their talents and interests so that they can discover other purposes.

As our daily purposes change, we may experience disappointment and hardship when we fall short of our hopes and expectations. But spiritual growth often emanates from our effort, not from our success. Just as each of us is unique, so are our journeys. As Amor Towles writes in his wonderful novel *A Gentleman in Moscow*:

> "What matters in life is not whether we receive a round of applause; what matters is whether we have the courage to venture forth despite the uncertainty of acclaim."

And if for today we experience a setback, the spiritual traditions of Judaism and Alcoholics Anonymous remind us that tomorrow is another opportunity to do better.

YOU ARE ENOUGH

It is human nature to imagine ourselves hitting the winning home run in a World Series, developing a cure for a horrible disease, receiving nightly applause for our acting or singing, or doing something else that makes us stand out from the crowd. But we are enough when our daily purpose reflects our unique talents and passions. We then live decently, because we are right-sized and for today we are in the right place, even if we may want to be in a different place tomorrow.

Whenever I am inclined to doubt whether I am enough, I recall the attitude of oil industrialist John D. Rockefeller. In the first part of the twentieth century, Rockefeller was one of the wealthiest people on earth. One day, a journalist asked Rockefeller, "How do you know when you have enough money?" Rockefeller replied, "When I have a little more than I do now." To paraphrase the great Green Bay Packers coach Vince Lombardi, Rockefeller's statement epitomizes an attitude that self-interest is not the most important thing, it is the only thing. Financially, Rockefeller may have been one of the richest people in the world, but at the moment that he made this remark, spiritually he may have been one of the poorest. I live with spiritual buoyancy because by using my talents and interests to live with a daily purpose that is uniquely mine, I know that I am enough.

A TORAH DRASH

Making Sense of the Census

The translation of the *parsha Ki Tissa* is "when you count." The portion begins with a census, an enumeration of every person among the Israelite people who left Egypt. This seems like one of the most boring and meaningless portions of the Torah. What is the purpose of identifying each person who left Egypt? Why aren't we given an estimate, or even an exact total, rather than an interminable individual accounting? This Torah portion teaches me that everyone is unique. Everyone matters! A total count, or a listing of the tribes that were represented, would ignore the fact that every person who left Egypt was a unique individual. The Torah reminds us that each of us must see ourselves as a unique individual with a unique role to play in making our families and our communities better.

SHARES FROM THE SHUV: EMBRACING OUR UNIQUE DAILY PURPOSE

A Musician's Unique Melody
A Friend

I am an alcoholic, a musician and a former resident of Beit T'Shuvah. Before entering Beit T'Shuvah I had spent more than a decade as a member of various bands. But if my pre-recovery career had been an infant, it would have been labeled "failure to thrive."

I loved both writing and performing, and when I started out as a musician I had my own unique musical style and "voice." But as I drifted from one band to another, I lost my voice. I always tried to please other band members, writing the kind of music that I thought fit their styles. To do this I often had to imitate the styles of other songwriters and performers. But nothing worked. The bands that I was in never progressed to bigger dates, clubs or venues, and eventually broke apart. As my failures mounted up I hated being a musician and my drinking problems increased. I became a blackout drunk. After a second DUI, a judge allowed me to serve part of my sentence at Beit T'Shuvah.

My experiences in recovery have taught me that I still love to write and perform music, but that for me to succeed I have to write songs that tell the stories that I want to tell in the way that I want to tell them. I can't compare my music or my success to that of other musicians. To maintain sobriety and live decently, I have to write and perform my own music to the best of my ability.

I can now genuinely appreciate my life even if I never become a hugely popular musician. I am slowly regaining my unique musical voice. I have had some success performing my own songs as a solo. I intend to join with a band soon because I enjoy the camaraderie that a band provides. But I have learned that it is not healthy for me to abandon my approach to music just to fit into a group. I will join together only with bandmates whose musical spirits align with mine.

Fit for Life
Amy G.

I cannot blame my addiction on a lousy childhood. My parents have enjoyed a marriage that has endured for more than thirty years and counting, and I have a loving sister. In college I was a four-time scholar/athlete, participating in Division 1 soccer, cross-country and track and field. I graduated on the Dean's List with a B.A. in Sociology and Business Management.

I also graduated with a stress fracture in my pelvis. I was prescribed opiates, and what was supposed to be temporary management of pain blossomed into full-blown addiction. While I worked full time in the fitness industry, I fought my addiction by enrolling in an outpatient program. I managed to abstain from opiates for a year, until I injured my neck. Opiates were prescribed for me, and I was quickly hooked on them again. From opiates I moved on to smoking heroin, and I turned into an out-of-control heroin addict. I had a massive identity crisis. I was lost and lonely, and I did not know what my purpose in life was.

After an intervention organized by my family, I agreed to go to Beit T'Shuvah. I poured every ounce of my being into the recovery program, and rediscovered my passion for health and fitness. As the coordinator of Beit T'Shuvah's Mind and Body program, I am able to walk my talk. I teach residents how to reconnect to their bodies in sobriety through mindfulness, a healthy diet, exercise and yoga. I am so grateful to Beit T'Shuvah. I have renewed my connection to God, and more importantly, to myself. I have a new pair of eyes, a renewed heart, and a new life of purpose.

If It Saves One Life
Andrea S-B

My husband and I are grateful members of the Beit T'Shuvah community. Some years ago we proposed to Rabbi Mark an Externship program to support Beit T'Shuvah's mission of re-kindling residents' passion for living with purpose. Our idea was to use contributions to the Externship program to pay stipends to residents who by working part-time would experience the satisfaction of living with daily purpose. We figured that if the money for the stipends came from Beit T'Shuvah, the result would be a larger pool of employers willing to take on residents who often had less-than-spotless records. We told Rabbi Mark that our main concern was that money directed to the Externship program might detract from Beit T'Shuvah's ability to pay for its other worthy programs. But Rabbi Mark enthusiastically supported our Externship proposal. He told us not to worry about the money, because "if the Externship program can save one life, it's worth it."

The Externship program continues to thrive. The part-time job opportunities it has created have helped many newly-sober residents experience the satisfaction of living with daily purpose. We are especially grateful that after moving out of the house, many residents have transformed their externships into full-time employment.

Back to School
Richard J.

I am not an addict; I learned about Beit T'Shuvah through the experiences of relatives. I assumed that Rabbi Mark's program for living with decency and purpose was for addicts and had no relevance to my life. But when I learned about his commitment to pursue his unique purpose and seek to become the best version of himself that he could, I realized that the commitment encompassed a life-changing decision that I had made about thirty years ago.

At that time, I had just graduated from divinity school and was about to accept a position as an assistant minister in a Presbyterian church. I did not grow up in a religious family, but starting in high school I developed a strong interest in studying comparative religion. After I graduated from college, I enrolled in divinity school both to continue my religious studies and because I thought that as a minister, I could use the church's religious beliefs and practices to build community and help parishioners.

Just as I was about to accept my first job as an assistant minister, my life took a U-turn. I thought about how much I had enjoyed my experiences as a volunteer tutor of elementary school children while I was in college and divinity school. I decided that my real purpose in life was to work with children as a schoolteacher. I called the minister, thanked him for the wonderful job offer, and told him that I had decided to teach. I went back to college for a year to obtain a teaching credential, and then became an upper elementary and middle school teacher. While I might have had a rewarding career as a minister, I knew that my real calling was to teach. And just as Rabbi Mark teaches residents of Beit T'Shuvah, before I retired I often talked to my students about how each of them is a unique blend of talents and interests, and that each of them can live well and contribute to the world in a way that no one else can. I know that people who suffer from addiction face challenges that non-addicts do not. But life is challenging for all of us, and the commitment to value what makes us unique is a lesson that we all need to learn.

Coming Full Circle
A Friend

I was paroled to Beit T'Shuvah after serving seven years in state prison. I grew up in a nominally Jewish home, but my family wasn't observant. When

I was in high school I felt lost. I didn't know where I fit in, except that I did not want to be anything like my parents. I drifted from one group to another, and I dressed, talked and acted like whatever group I was part of.

My addiction issues began when I left high school without graduating and started hanging out with a street gang. I stayed away from home for days at a time, and when I was home I was usually high and I ignored my parents. They kicked me out of the house and changed the locks to the doors, but I managed to sneak in when they weren't home and steal enough things that I could sell to support my drug habit. Soon I was dealing drugs and I gave birth to a daughter when I was twenty years old. When my daughter was four years old, I was convicted of drug dealing and went to prison. My parents refused to take care of her, so my daughter was raised in a foster home. My life was at a dead end; I didn't care if I spent the rest of it in prison.

Just to give myself something to do while in prison I started attending A.A. meetings. I found myself connecting to the stories so I decided to attend meetings that the Jewish prison chaplain led every couple of weeks. The meetings were the first time I had ever really tried to figure out who I was and what I could do with my life. I discovered that I wanted to live, and that I could give purpose to my life by working with young women who were as lost as I had been. I became anxious to get out of prison as soon as possible, and I did whatever it took to earn an early parole date.

The prison chaplain had put me in touch with Beit T'Shuvah, so I had a place to go when I was paroled. When I became a resident, I already had a plan for taking care of others and myself. I graduated from high school and I am now taking classes to be a drug counselor. I have reconnected with my parents; my daughter and I live with them. I am amazed and grateful for a life that I never thought I would have.

Back to Work
Josh R.

I have a law degree from the University of Detroit. After graduating I was sober for three years. At that point I became addicted to painkillers and heroin, and my addictions continued for years. I struggled to get well many times, but was never able to stay sober for more than a few weeks at a time. Despite my education, I felt incapable, alone and worthless. When my mom died I made a commitment to get well. I moved from Michigan to become a resident in Beit T'Shuvah and this changed my life. I am an intern in Beit

T'Shuvah's Development department and I love the supportive people I work with. I receive a stipend, but far more important to me is that I enjoy a life of daily purpose. I have re-captured my sense of self-esteem, confidence and drive. I don't know where my career will take me but I am passionate about the work I do today. I know that the path I follow from here will be uniquely mine.

My Joy of Cooking
Julie B.

My life at age twenty-seven was great. I had six siblings and the greatest parents anyone could wish for, and I managed three multi-million dollar salons. But when I found out that my mom had suddenly died in her sleep, I fell into a deep depression. I started to numb my pain with pills, and over the next five years my life fell apart. When I finally admitted that I needed help, Beit T'Shuvah was there for me. I gave the program everything I had, and after a few months had enough recovery to become an intern in the kitchen. That led to my current job as the Shuv's kitchen manager. I get to do what I love every day, cooking and helping residents learn to cook. I love watching them being creative, having fun and feeling part of the community. I realize that all of us have trials and tribulations, and what matters is how we handle them. Beit T'Shuvah saved my life and gave me a job that allows me to live with a joyful sense of purpose every day.

CHAPTER NINE

SEVENTH COMMITMENT

I will not adulterate my soul; I will observe boundaries instead of seeking to control the actions of others.

THE SEVENTH COMMANDMENT forbids adultery. The prohibition of sexual activity outside the marital relationship encloses married couples in imaginary circles. Each imaginary circle creates a firm boundary that legitimizes sexual activity for the couple inside the circle while forbidding sexual activity between a person who is inside a circle with another person who is outside.

My corollary seventh spiritual commitment is to draw an imaginary circle around myself and abstain from trying to control the actions of anyone outside that circle. I am responsible only for the actions of the one person who is inside the circle: me. Through this commitment I act in harmony with my understanding that people are holy souls who are endowed with free will and entitled to the dignity of their own choices.

THE SERENITY PRAYER

This seventh commitment embraces the spiritual principles of the Serenity Prayer, which is central to Alcoholics Anonymous and all other Twelve Step programs. The Serenity Prayer goes as follows:

God, grant me the serenity
To accept the things I cannot change,

The courage to change the things I can.
And the wisdom to know the difference.

The Serenity Prayer helps me to accept the reality that the behavior and choices of other people are things that I cannot change. The Serenity Prayer reminds me that observing boundaries is not a personal choice; it is a spiritual obligation. When I refrain from telling people that their plans are mistaken, and from offering my advice on what they should do, I implicitly communicate my confidence: "I know that you are capable of deciding what the next right action is for you to take. And if it turns out that you made a mistake, I know that you have the capacity to make amends and learn from it so that you won't repeat the mistake in the future." Observing boundaries is not a chore. It is a spiritual expression of confidence and respect.

THE INNER PHARAOH

Jewish tradition recounts the period when Egyptian Pharaohs enslaved the Jews. But a Pharaoh is not only a ruler of ancient Egypt. If within each of us dwells a spark of holiness, in my understanding then within each of us dwells a Pharaoh too. My inner Pharaoh reveals itself in my urge to try to control the behavior of others by telling them what I think they ought to do. Through this commitment I wrestle with this urge and do my best not to give unsolicited advice. Unless somebody asks for my advice, I zip my lip. For instance, I don't try to influence people's career choices, tell people who I think have acted wrongly that they need to make amends, or tell residents what kinds of careers I think they ought to pursue after they move out of "the house." As much as I may tell myself that I know what is best for other people, I have to be humble. I cannot predict the future nor can I understand "the whole truth" of another person's unique circumstances, talents and interests. A decision that would be wrong for me might be correct for somebody else, and a decision that seems wrong to me today might prove to be correct tomorrow. For both pragmatic and spiritual reasons, unless and until a person asks me for help or advice I observe boundaries by keeping my mouth shut.

Even when I am asked for advice I may hold off giving it if the person asking for it is fully capable of figuring out the next right action. Not long ago, I spoke to a woman who had been a Beit T'Shuvah resident for about six months. Because of repeated relapses, she had spent much of the prior few years in a variety of other residential rehabs. She came to talk to me because she was anxious to move out and go home, but realized that if she was going to avoid yet another relapse she needed to leave with a plan for her next step in place. When she came into my office, she said, "Rabbi, I feel good and I'm really ready to go home. But I'm not sure what to do after I leave here. What do you think I ought to do?" Rather than give her advice, I told her, "I can't tell you what to do. I agree with you that you should not move out without having a plan of action in place. But only you can know what you are passionate about, and what will help you realize that you matter and that you can live with a unique daily purpose that nobody else can. Sorry, but you'll have to figure it out." She came back to my office a few days later and told me how much she appreciated Beit T'Shuvah's counselors. She wanted to be a counselor who could help other people with addiction problems not suffer as much as she had. A few days later she moved out and Beit T'Shuvah hired her as a counseling intern. Soon afterwards she enrolled in a school program leading to a Certificate as a Drug and Alcohol Counselor. By not doing for the resident what she was capable of doing for herself, I gave her the space to take an important step towards a richer and more meaningful life and a realization that she was capable of making her own decisions.

RHETORICAL QUESTIONS

My commitment to observing boundaries extends to refraining from trying to provide unsolicited advice in the guise of rhetorical questions. Rhetorical questions can beguile me into telling myself that I am not providing unsolicited advice, rather I am only trying to make sure that a person has thought through a scenario carefully before acting.

For example, the parent of an addict might tell me that she has decided to continue to support a child financially, despite the child's continued substance abuse and unwillingness to look for a job. Were the parent to ask me for advice, I might say something along the lines of, "I think you are making a serious mistake. You are trying to show love, but in reality you are crippling your child by enabling the child to continue the addictive behavior without experiencing its consequences." Rather than be such an obvious Pharaoh, if the parent did not ask for my advice I might instead ask the parent a series of rhetorical questions. For example, I might ask questions such as, "If you continue your support, will your child be motivated to stop using and find a job?" "Do you demonstrate love when you do for your child what your child should do for himself?" Rhetorical questions such as these are in reality slow forms of offering unsolicited advice. Questions such as these violate my commitment to give people the dignity of their own thinking.

"BOTH/AND" ADVICE

As a rabbi and especially in a place like Beit T'Shuvah, I am often asked for my advice. And when I am, I try to use a simple "both/and" approach to advice-giving that allows me to respond to requests for advice *and* to respect boundaries. I offer guidance and refer to the experiences and values on which my guidance is based. This approach allows advice-seekers to evaluate the wisdom of my advice by comparing their experiences and values to mine.

For example, not long ago a Beit T'Shuvah resident who was about to move out of "the house" asked me whether she should try to re-connect with an aunt who had wanted nothing to do with her during the years that she was actively in her disease. The resident was fearful of how she would react if the aunt continued to reject her after she had gotten sober. I responded by telling her, "I think it is important for you to try to re-connect with her and make amends because family members who are there for you can sustain you when times are rough. Your aunt may still not want a relationship with you. But even so, I think you will feel better about yourself for knowing that you have done all you can to demonstrate to your aunt that she matters to you." I hoped that my "both/and" response gave the resident a chance to evaluate the wisdom of my advice by comparing my values and experiences to hers. If she decided that she would feel worse rather than better about herself if her aunt rejected her attempt to make amends, the resident had a basis for behaving differently than I might have in the same situation.

CHOOSING LIFE

In the Jewish tradition, my ultimate obligation as a human being is to choose life. For example, in my understanding of the tradition even an observant Jew who is ordinarily mandated to abstain from eating on Yom Kippur has an obligation to eat if a serious medical condition requires regular nourishment. In the same way, my commitment to observe boundaries by refusing to give unsolicited advice must give way when a person's plans risk serious harm to themselves or others.

One such scenario arises when a resident with only a short period of sobriety plans to go out with friends with whom he used to drink and use. The high risk of relapse and other serious consequences may lead me to advise against going out and to urge the resident to talk to a sponsor or other friend in recovery. I recognize that an overly liberal interpretation of the risk of harm can interfere with my commitment to observe boundaries. As with any other situation, I have to do my best to act righteously through such actions as wrestling with my conflicting desires to be selfish and selfless, examining my motives, telling myself the truth and seeking help from others if I am uncertain of what to do.

A TORAH DRASH

Knowing Our Place

In the *parsha Masei*, before the Israelites enter the Promised Land, God describes the inheritance of nine-and-a-half of the twelve tribes of Israel to Moses. (The other two and a half tribes had already received their goodies.) God comes across here as an extremely professional surveyor. The western boundary is to be the coast of the Mediterranean Sea. But Moses has to establish the northern boundary by running a line from the Mediterranean Sea to Mount Hor, then to Lebo Hamath, then to Zedad and Ziphron, and ending at Hazar Enan.

God's careful identification of landmarks demonstrates the importance of "knowing our place." Physical boundaries prevent chaos by distinguishing the space that we are responsible to care for from the spaces that are the responsibility of others. When we differentiate the decisions that are ours to make from those that are better left to other people we create healthy emotional and spiritual boundaries. We prevent chaos by deciding on our next right actions while respecting the right of others to make the decisions that they think best.

SHARES FROM THE SHUV: OBSERVING BOUNDARIES

It'll Be Good For You: Part One
A Friend

I am an alcoholic who has had trouble maintaining sobriety. Beit T'Shuvah was the fifth rehab I had been to, and I was a resident for nearly a year before my treatment team and I decided that my recovery was strong enough for me to move to a sober living house. But even after I moved out of "the house," I stayed connected to Beit T'Shuvah by attending meetings and many Friday night services.

One of my cousins was to be married about three months after I moved into the sober living house. It was to be a large wedding attended by virtually all members of my family. I was thrilled for my cousin but as the wedding date drew closer, I became increasingly anxious about attending. I knew that alcohol would be flowing liberally and I was worried about jeopardizing the best period of recovery I had ever had.

When I told my parents that I did not want to attend the wedding, they urged me to go. They pointed out that my relapses had often occurred when I isolated myself, and that going to the wedding would be good for me, that it would help me to feel good about my life. While they didn't say this, I also knew that they didn't want to be embarrassed and ashamed in front of their family members by having their daughter be the only close family member who was absent from the wedding. Somewhat reluctantly, I did attend the wedding. I acted as if I was comfortable and had only non-alcoholic drinks. Afterwards, my parents and a couple of other relatives who knew of my struggles with sobriety told me how proud of me they were.

However, within a week of the wedding I suffered another relapse. Despite my outward appearance and the presence of so many people I genuinely cared for, I had felt very alone and scared at the wedding. I became increasingly anxious and depressed as I compared my life to the lives of other family members, and despite my determination to stay sober I took a drink. Fortunately, before I hit another bottom I reached out to Beit T'Shuvah and was allowed to return for another six-month period of residency. I am again in a sober living house and for today I am clean and sober.

I later learned from Rabbi Mark that he had known of my parents' efforts to convince me to attend the wedding. He told me that his personal opinion had been that I was not yet far enough along in my recovery to subject myself to the stress of attending a large wedding. He would have told me, "You can't save your ass and your parents' faces at the same time." But as I had not asked for his advice, he had not offered it. While I was initially upset by Rabbi Mark's failure to advise me not to attend the wedding, I ultimately was grateful for his silence. I have to learn to be responsible for my own decisions. I made a mistake, but I am stronger for the experience and better able to deal with life on life's terms as a result.

It'll Be Good For You: Part Two
A Friend

We are the parents of a daughter who was a resident of Beit T'Shuvah. All of us were invited to a large family wedding that took place about three months after our daughter had moved out of Beit T'Shuvah and into a sober living apartment. She was doing well in recovery and had a part-time job. However, she was reluctant to attend the wedding, because she just wasn't sure she would be comfortable and feel that she belonged there.

As the wedding date approached, we urged our daughter to attend. We told her that it would be good for her to be part of a happy event with the rest of the family, including the many aunts, uncles and cousins she had always felt close to. We knew that alcohol would be plentiful, but we pointed out that non-alcoholic drinks would also be served and that it would also be good for her to realize that she could remain sober in a party atmosphere.

Our daughter did attend the wedding, and unfortunately she relapsed about a week later. Initially we were upset with our daughter for her inability to stay sober. But when we thought about the part we had played in her relapse, we were upset with ourselves. Beit T'Shuvah gave her another chance, and we visited her there to make amends.

Before the wedding, we had convinced ourselves that going to the wedding would be good for our daughter. Now we apologized to her for not being honest with her or ourselves that we wanted her to be at the wedding so that we wouldn't feel embarrassed and ashamed in front of so many close members of our family by having an alcoholic child who was afraid to attend. We apologized to our daughter for not trusting her judgment. We told her that while we could not erase our conduct or her relapse, our plan for the future was to do our best to restore the trust that we had damaged by giving her the dignity of her own thinking. We also promised not to give her advice that she hadn't asked for, not even through the guise of questioning her decisions through a series of rhetorical questions along the lines of, "Have you considered this?" and "Have you considered that?" Today our daughter is doing well in recovery and we have done our best to live up to our promises to her to keep our noses out of her life.

Broken Boundaries
Claire N.

I moved to Connecticut from California many years ago. Other family members, including my closest relative Aunt Esther, continued to live in California. During a five year period, while my aged aunt suffered increased dementia, I made an astounding thirty-nine trips to Los Angeles in response to frequent phone calls from her or her friends regarding the quality of her care or her physical condition. The airfare and related costs of travel ate up a significant amount of my savings. By the time my Aunt Esther passed away, I was in my mid-sixties and personally and financially exhausted. I diminished my life by ignoring my own needs in order to see to hers and acting as though I didn't matter. Now in my mid-seventies and at a time when I expected to be retired, I still have to work to pay off the debts I incurred trying to take care of my aunt.

Tough Love
A Friend

I am a single mom whose son was addicted to powerful painkillers. For a while I let him live with me in the hope that my love and attention would heal him. Instead he sat around the apartment most days, stayed out all night and repeatedly trashed both the apartment and me. When he started stealing money from my purse and pawning objects from my house, I finally had enough. I told him he had to leave, and I changed the locks on my doors.

My son couch-surfed for as long as he could, until no one would take him in. A few months after I kicked him out, I learned that he spent his days on the streets and his nights in a storage room in a derelict warehouse. I knew he couldn't come back to live with me, but I was terrified that he would die. So I started bringing him food, and once in a while I would clean the storage room. Whenever I saw him he was clearly high, and I didn't ask how he was able to afford his drug habit. But I thought that if I kept him alive, he would come to his senses and agree to enter rehab.

Joining the Beit T'Shuvah community and attending Al-Anon meetings helped me to realize that my actions were enabling my son to survive as a homeless drug addict. I found the strength to tell him that I would no longer feed him or clean the storage room. Occasionally, my son would knock on my door and ask for a meal and a shower. Without letting him in, I would ask if he was ready to go to rehab, and when he would refuse I would tell him to go away. Sometimes I would toss a pillow and a blanket out of the front door, then quickly close and lock it. I never imagined motherhood would be this way. It broke my heart to see my son sleeping under a tree. But I didn't know what else to do.

After a few more months, my gaunt and barely recognizable son came to my door and said that he needed and wanted help. I so wanted my son to contact Beit T'Shuvah, even though we are not Jewish. My son finally made the phone call, and Beit T'Shuvah agreed that he could start as a day patient and we would go from there. My son showed his willingness by going to Beit T'Shuvah every day, and when a bed opened up he became a resident. I couldn't force my son to change, but through my changed actions my son was able to develop the courage to change his behavior.

Fear Strikes Out
A Friend

I had been a resident of Beit T'Shuvah for a couple of months when I got a pass to go out to dinner with my parents. Before we had gotten very far we got into a big argument. I asked about the family trip that we had been planning before I went into rehab, and when they told me that they had decided to postpone it I was furious. In retrospect I know that they did the right thing, but in the moment I screamed at them that they didn't trust me. When we stopped for a red light I opened the car door, jumped out and ran away down the sidewalk.

I ran in the direction of Beit T'Shuvah, but I had to pass by a couple of liquor and convenience stores to get there. I figured that my parents would be so terrified that I would buy or steal liquor from one of them that they would turn the car around and come after me. But they didn't; they just drove off and went out to eat by themselves. Looking back I am so grateful that my parents didn't try to rescue me that day. They were fearful, but they gave me the dignity of my own thinking and allowed me to be responsible for my own actions. I didn't buy or use alcohol; I walked directly back to Beit

T'Shuvah and calmed down with the help of the community. Today I have an amazing life-my family is back in my life and I have a good job. I know that my parents' decision to observe boundaries and refrain from acting on their fear that evening helped make this possible.

CHAPTER TEN

EIGHTH COMMITMENT

I will not steal from my own soul; I will augment its strength by nurturing spiritual partnerships.

T HE EIGHTH COMMANDMENT instructs us not to steal. I understand the commandment to refer to two forms of theft: *Crimes* of theft typically involve the stealing of money or property. *Spiritual* theft involves respect and dignity. We disrespect others and steal from their dignity when we take unfair advantage of their weaknesses, ignore their cries for help or spread hurtful gossip. Spiritual theft may not be punishable by law but its consequences can be as severe as illegal forms of theft.

My corollary eighth spiritual commitment is to respect the dignity of my soul and strengthen my impulse to act righteously by nurturing spiritual partnerships. My spiritual partners help me wrestle with my conflicting desires to act selfishly and selflessly in the pursuit of right actions. Through my connections to spiritual partners I live in community, so that I never have to experience the joys and sorrows of life alone. Living in community reminds me that in the words of my friend Reverend Mark Whitlock, because "we are all kin under the skin," more than my personal well-being is at stake in all of my actions.

SPIRITUAL PARTNERSHIPS

American mythology celebrates "rugged individualism." But for the two decades when my actions were controlled by my addictions, I was a "ragged" rather than a "rugged" individual. I was trapped in one of the most dangerous places for me to live: the isolation of my own mind. My experiences have taught me that I can enjoy a richer and more meaningful life by helping and receiving help from spiritual partners. Spiritual partners augment my impulse to act righteously because I am accountable to my spiritual partners for my actions, and they are accountable to me for theirs.

My spiritual partnerships of course reflect the uniqueness of my life. My most intimate and crucial spiritual partner is my wife Harriet. Her love and support and that of the members of my family have helped me remain sober and in recovery for nearly thirty years. My spiritual partnerships with Harriet, my daughter Heather and my brother Neal provide serenity because I know that I don't have to do life alone. We can turn to each other for help with any personal or professional matter.

While I am ultimately responsible for my actions as Beit T'Shuvah's spiritual leader, I try to learn how to be a better spiritual leader through my partnerships with my mentor Rabbi Ed Feinstein and other clerical colleagues such as Father Greg Boyle and Reverend Mark Whitlock.

To further my understanding of the spiritual traditions of Judaism, Alcoholics Anonymous and other religious and spiritual traditions, I maintain spiritual partnerships with Beit T'Shuvah residents, alumni, employees, congregants and other people who enjoy studying and discussing texts such as the Torah and the Talmud.

My spiritual partners also include the writers of religious and secular texts that speak to my soul. Primary among these writers is Rabbi Abraham Joshua Heschel; others include Rabbi Heschel's daughter Susannah, the Reverend Martin Luther King, and sociologist Erich Fromm. Writers such as these inspire me with their words to such an extent that I seem to be in conversation with them as I read. (Admittedly, often these silent inner conversations turn into arguments! What can I say, I'm Jewish!)

And of course Beit T'Shuvah, the organization made up of changing but always wonderfully crazy people that saved my life and has saved so many others, is also a spiritual partner. The dedication and creative spirit of the entire community sustains my impulse to act righteously and my hope for a world in which all people can overcome their spiritual maladies and live richer and more meaningful lives.

Spiritual partnerships inevitably reflect the imperfections of the partners. I don't always agree with my spiritual partners' actions, and I assure you that they don't always agree with mine. We can argue; we can get angry; and we can sometimes act badly towards each other. But reactions such as these are not shameful. They are ways of assuring each other that we care and that our relationship matters. *Sing Out,* a lovely poem by the Jewish writer Aaron Zeitlin echoes the idea that even disagreement is a form of spiritual connection. The poem begins with the verses:

Praise me says God, I will know that you love me.
Curse me, says God, I will know that you love me.
And ends with the verses:
If you don't praise and don't revile,
Then I created you in vain, says God.

These words remind me that we steal from our soul's impulse to act righteously when we embrace isolation rather than connection. Whether we offer praise or criticism, when we offer it with compassion and a caring purpose we stimulate ourselves and others to take the next right action.

For example, I meet almost weekly with my mentor and friend Rabbi Ed Feinstein to discuss our thoughts about the Torah portions for upcoming Friday night services. Though our interpretations of a Torah portion and the makeup of our congregations may be very different, we are spiritual partners because we want to help each other understand the text from our unique perspectives. We want to help each other be present so that each of us can speak from our soul, for no matter how we might have understood a Torah portion previously our spiritual commitment to our congregations is to explore what the Torah teaches us in the moment. I can ask Rabbi Ed for help because I am not afraid to let him see that I will never be as learned in Jewish texts as he is. Rabbi Ed can ask me for help because he is not afraid to let me see that my perspectives growing out of my immersion in the recovery community can broaden his understanding of Jewish texts. We are spiritual partners when we ask each other for help, for in this way we say to each other, "I cannot do this on my own, and you don't have to do this on your own either." We don't always end up in agreement about the meaning of the text we study, but through our mutual willingness to reach out to each other we each know that we matter.

Spiritual partnerships help us to prevent the unique maladies of our souls from controlling our actions. Our spiritual partners cannot prevent bad things from befalling us; disappointment, illness and loss are among the inevitable consequences of being alive. But they can help us stay right-sized and help us to keep putting one foot in front of the other so that we can retain our dignity and continue to do our best to act righteously. In the Jewish tradition, healing doesn't consist of *getting* better, because sometimes we don't get better. We heal by *acting* better, showing up and responding with strength and dignity when misfortune and sadness confront us. Spiritual partnerships help us to *heal Jewishly.*

The life-affirming power of spiritual partnerships is poignantly illustrated by a short remembrance written by a German pastor named Martin Niemöller during the rise of the Nazis in 1930's Germany. Pastor Niemöller told of how he remained silent when the Nazis eliminated communities of which he was not a part, such as Socialists and Jews. When the Nazis finally came for him, no community remained to speak up for him.

Pastor Niemöller's eloquent words testify to the destructiveness of caring only about ourselves and ignoring our common humanity. His remembrance teaches us that we steal from our own dignity when we forget that we are all kin and when we allow ourselves to stand idly by while others suffer. We augment our soul when we join with spiritual partners to demonstrate concern and compassion for the needs and desires of all human beings. As Rabbi Abraham Joshua Heschel taught us, to live with care and concern for community is to engage in being human; rather than simply existing as a human being.

OUR NEED FOR HELP

In the wonderful musical film *Chicago,* Velma Kelly sings about her need for a partner for her dance act: "You may think there's nothing to it, but I simply cannot do it… alone." The song's lyrics apply equally to the quest for a richer and more meaningful life. We simply cannot do it alone. We all need help. I had always equated a need for help with weakness. But I have come to recognize that one of the greatest of human strengths is the willingness to ask for and accept help from spiritual partners. Our willingness to ask for help means that we can accept our imperfections and our inability to see more than part of the truth. We can ask for help when we are willing to be *visible* to our spiritual partners, inviting them to see our imperfections, our fears, our limitations and our mistakes. When we feel lost, broken or uncertain, our connections to spiritual partners mean that we always have a community of people to whom we can turn for help.

We can also maintain spiritual partnerships with our own souls. Prayer, meditation and spiritual inventories provide spaces for us to connect our conscious mind to our inner spark of holiness. Margaret Fishback Powers illustrates this type of spiritual partnership beautifully in her poem, *Footprints in the Sand*. The poem describes images of life that arise in a dreamer's mind as the dreamer walks along a dark and secluded beach. Two sets of footprints are in each image, one belonging to the dreamer and one to God. Looking back at the sets of footprints after the last image has passed, the dreamer notices that at the saddest times of the dreamer's life there was but one set of footprints. The dreamer asks, "Lord, why did you desert me when I most needed your help?" The Lord responds to the dreamer, "When you saw only one set of footprints, it was then that I carried you." As in the poem, we never have to do life alone. When we create private moments to connect our conscious mind to our subconscious impulse to act righteously, we can live richer and more meaningful lives.

HINEINI: "HERE I AM"

In the Jewish tradition, God calls to the patriarch Abraham and Abraham answers, *Hineini*: "Here I am." We form spiritual partnerships by emulating Abraham and responding with "*Hineini*" whenever people seek help from us. Whether the request comes from a family member or a friend, or is a cry for help from the widow, the poor, the orphan or the stranger, we act righteously when we say "*Hineini*." We also say "*Hineini*" when we accept amends from people who have wronged or harmed us. When we are of service to others, we matter and we assure others that they matter too.

Just as with individuals, spiritual communities have an obligation to say "*Hineini*" to each other. When the leader of an organization that provides services from a different faith tradition for a population that is similar to Beit T'Shuvah's told me that his organization was in financial distress, Beit T'Shuvah said "*Hineini*." For several weeks, congregants at Beit T'Shuvah's Friday night services gave a portion of their donations (which ordinarily are used to defray the costs of weekend events that help residents learn how to have fun in sobriety) to the other organization. Congregants even increased their contributions significantly during this period of time, so that as a community we could say "*Hineini*" not only to the other community but also to our own residents. Thanks in small part to Beit T'Shuvah's help, the organization continues to thrive.

The service traditions of Alcoholics Anonymous and Beit T'Shuvah also teach people to grow spiritually by saying *"Hineini."* Alcoholics Anonymous teaches that whenever any addict anywhere reaches out for help, that person is a spiritual partner whom people in recovery are responsible to help. Beit T'Shuvah and Twelve Step groups depend on the willingness of members to say *"Hineini"* by accepting voluntary service commitments. Commitments in Twelve Step groups range from leading meetings to sponsoring other addicts to making coffee at and cleaning up a room after meetings. At Beit T'Shuvah, residents' service tasks include helping to serve and clean up after meals; cleaning hallways; taking other residents to meetings outside the house; and welcoming congregants to Friday night services. But whether their tasks are large or small, the people who do service are the principal beneficiaries of their righteous acts. When we learn to say *"Hineini,"* we show up for life and demonstrate that each of us matters.

FITTING IN

Our uniqueness as human beings sustains the strength of spiritual partnerships, whether they consist of two individuals or large communities. For example, Beit T'Shuvah and Alcoholics Anonymous groups do not sustain themselves as spiritual communities because all addicts are alike. They sustain themselves as spiritual communities because individuals are willing to contribute their unique and diverse talents, interests and passions to the common goals of healing, living decently and acting righteously.

Spiritual partnerships remind me of a jigsaw puzzle: each piece of a jigsaw puzzle is unique and it fits in only one place. So too is it with us humans. We can get lost when we try to contort ourselves and hide what makes us unique in an effort to "fit in" to places we don't belong. When we are where we belong, we fit and we make our spiritual partnerships and the whole world better, stronger and more usable.

A SPIRITUAL WORLD COMMUNITY? IMAGINE!

In one of his most beautiful and poignant songs, John Lennon asked us to "Imagine all the people, living life in peace." Lennon admitted in the song that he was a dreamer. I dream along with Lennon because the dream itself nourishes my hope that one day at a time each of us will become a grain of sand more willing to think of everyone else as part of a world spiritual community. I understand that this dream may never become reality—certainly not in my lifetime or anything close to it. But I do my best to act righteously with the hope that someday all the peoples of the earth will become a single spiritual community, doing their best to live well and to help others to live well.

Unfortunately the expansion of human knowledge and the growth of technology that we in this generation are privileged to enjoy has not been accompanied by a commensurate reduction in character traits such as greed, envy, hatred and intolerance. But my own spiritual journey out of the darkness into the light proves that the impulse to act selfishly can never fully extinguish the spiritual pilot light of the impulse to act selflessly. I feel the potential for our inner spark of holiness to lead to the development of a more unified world when members of Alcoholics Anonymous gather together to help each other maintain sobriety by sharing their experience, strength and hope; when Jews gather together at a Passover Seder to remind themselves of the continuing presence and evil of slavery by telling the story of the ancient Hebrews' escape from bondage under Pharaoh; when Father Greg Boyle of Homeboy Industries seeks to reduce violence and foster mutual self-respect by helping members of rival street gangs learn how to live decently and work together; when Muslims seek to promote peace and understanding by bowing down together towards Mecca to acknowledge their allegiance to Allah; and when people raise money and sometimes risk their lives to protect the lives of refugees who are victims of oppression or torture.

Temporary and enduring spiritual communities of all sizes and types exist now, and God willing they have the potential to move human beings in the direction of a worldwide caring community in which people derive fulfillment from accepting help and saying *Hineini* when they are asked for help. In the faint but echoing voice of our inner spark of holiness we can at least imagine a world community that is committed to making the world a more compassionate and just place for all of its inhabitants.

A TORAH DRASH

Enter a Plea

The *parsha Va'etchanan* translates to "and he pleaded." In this portion of the Torah, Moses pleads with God for the opportunity to enter the Land of Canaan with the Israelites. He is unsuccessful; despite leading the Jews through the desert for forty years he never enters the land of Israel.

This Torah portion leads me to ask myself the question, "What am I pleading for?" This is a wonderful question for all of us. Pleading is an acknowledgment of our need for help, an acknowledgement that in isolation we are powerless, and an acknowledgement that when we plead for help we live in the solution rather than remaining stuck in the problem.

Rabbi Mark's App Store
Active Listening

I have to be an effective listener if I am to truly hear and respond to the people in my spiritual communities. Listening is more intense than simply hearing. In order to listen, I have to be focused and intentional. There are times when I am in dialogue with someone and I am not listening with intention and then all of a sudden I say, "What did you say?" The reason for this is that I had drifted away and then "woke up" when I heard something that did or did not make sense to me. I am in essence sleeping through a conversation. My commitment to engaging with caring communities includes a commitment to hearing and listening with intention and focus. In this way listening is the beginning of learning.

Active listening is a type of listening tool that helps me to engage spiritually with people who seek my help. By listening actively to a person who seeks my counsel, I try to create an emotional connection between us that promotes rapport and trust. Active listening responses allow me to demonstrate my concern for what a person says without judging the person or providing unwanted or at least premature advice. By actively listening, I also allow the people who seek my counsel to decide what information is pertinent to the problems or concerns that give rise to the conversation.

You are no doubt familiar with many so-called "passive listening" responses. For instance, I can listen passively to a person by conveying visual interest while remaining silent; by nodding my head; and by making non-committal responses such as "uh huh" or "please go on." These types of responses demonstrate my interest in the person I am talking with while also allowing the person to decide what to talk about.

Non-directive responses are "active" when they reflect back to speakers the emotions or sensations that appear to underlie their words. For example, suppose that a parent of a new resident tells me, "It's so hard for me to put my son into a drug rehab when almost all the other parents we know are getting ready to send their kids off to college." My active listening response might be, "You feel shame because your son won't start college at the same time as most of his friends." This response would reflect back the feeling (shame) that I think underlies the parent's remark. The response does not judge the parent's action: "Don't worry, you're doing the right thing." Nor do I provide unwarranted advice: "Trust me, you'll feel better about this in a few weeks."

I was initially very reluctant to embrace active listening. Active listening responses sounded artificial to me, and I thought that the people I talked to would spot them immediately and clam up rather than talk openly and honestly. My fears were unfounded. No one has ever reacted badly to an active listening response. And as I began to introduce these responses into emotion-arousing conversations, they ceased sounding strange to me. Using occasional active listening responses when appropriate makes me less likely to be judgmental or give premature advice, and more likely to allow the people I am talking with rather than me to decide what to talk about.

I always remember a conversation with Linda, a community college instructor who taught courses in communication skills to students who are interested in becoming therapists or counselors—including rabbis, priests and ministers. Linda taught active listening skills (along with other listening and conversational skills) through class discussions and role-play exercises.

Linda told me about her experience with a student named Darius. Darius was very vocal in his antagonism towards active listening. During an early class discussion, Darius said something like, "I will never use active listening. It sounds so phony, instead of motivating people to talk openly and honestly it will make them not want to talk with me at all."

In one of those priceless "teaching moments," Linda decided to try out an instant in-class demonstration of active listening. She sensed that underlying Darius' words were the emotions of hostility and fear. So she reflected one of these feelings back to him with an active listening response along the lines of, "Darius, sounds like there's something about active listening that you find scary." Darius responded by saying, "Darn right I do. I just think that if I try to use active listening, people will think that I'm a phony who is trying to manipulate them into saying what I want them to say. I think a lot of people will just stop talking and leave..." Linda told me how Darius suddenly stopped talking in mid-sentence. He realized that Linda's active listening response to his initial comment had motivated him to elaborate on it. All Darius could do was smile sheepishly and say, "Maybe I was wrong. Maybe active listening does work. I'll think about it."

SHARES FROM THE SHUV: SPIRITUAL PARTNERSHIPS

Running4Recovery
A Friend

I descended into the abyss of alcohol addiction even though I had a good career as an investment banker on Wall Street. Prior to becoming a resident of Beit T'Shuvah, I had been in and out of A.A. and had been to a number of outpatient clinics. On several occasions I had drunk so much that I had to detox in an emergency room. Once I even took pills in an effort to kill myself. In desperation I called my A.A. sponsor, who knew about Beit T'Shuvah and told me who to call.

After a few weeks in "the house" I joined Beit T'Shuvah's L.A. Marathon team, called Running4Recovery. It's the best thing I've ever done for myself. It helps me focus on a goal (making it to the finish line), and that helps me to set goals for staying sober. For the first time in my life I am part of a spiritual community in which we all support each other and help each other find a balance between pushing ourselves too hard and not doing the work we have to do to be able to run twenty-six miles. Before I came to Beit T'Shuvah, I was a broken soul who had no hope and no place to go. Now I have a bed and I am a part of the smaller marathon team spiritual community within the larger spiritual community that is Beit T'Shuvah. Connection to spiritual communities will forever be an important part of my sobriety and my life.

Not So Bad
A Friend

I am a heroin addict with a long history of failed attempts at recovery. Beit T'Shuvah was the fifteenth time I had been in treatment and for today it is my last one.

When I agreed to enter Beit T'Shuvah following yet another relapse, I did so just to get my family off my back. Most everyone who loved me had given up on me, and I figured I'd do one last unsuccessful stint in rehab and then never have to deal with anyone in my family again. I knew in my heart that I was a helpless and hopeless addict who would never be able to hold on to recovery.

I'll always remember that when I first met with Rabbi Mark, he asked me was to tell him about some of the good things I could remember doing. I thought he was crazy and I told him so: "Are you kidding? I've been a heroin addict for years. I'm a liar and a cheat. I haven't done a damn thing right."

But this jerk sitting in front of me who was unlike any rabbi or minister I'd ever met wouldn't accept my answer: "Come on, you're lying to me and you're lying to yourself. Tell me a few things that you're proud of doing." As I sat there in silence I actually started crying. I told him that I was proud that I had shown up clean and sober for my sister's wedding, and that during periods of sobriety I'd been a good sponsor to a few A.A. sisters.

In most of our conversations, Rabbi Mark pushed me to talk about what I'd had done right, either before I came to Beit T'Shuvah or during my residency there. I think this helped me to begin to think of myself as a decent person who had made a lot of mistakes and hurt a lot of people. I slowly began to see that I had the potential to live decently.

Ever since I left Beit T'Shuvah, I check in periodically with Rabbi Mark to tell him about a decent action that makes me particularly proud. Anyone else might think I was egotistical, but he and I know that this is a tool that helps me to live decently. The person who I once thought of as a jerk is now one of my spiritual partners!

CHAPTER ELEVEN

NINTH COMMITMENT

I will not lie to my own soul; I will tell myself the truth about my mistakes and misdeeds.

THE NINTH COMMANDMENT instructs us not to bear false witness against a neighbor. The commandment in my understanding speaks to the importance of truth-telling to the maintenance of a moral community, whether or not we are in a court of law and whether a person is geographically a "neighbor" or a stranger.

My corollary ninth spiritual commitment is to tell myself the truth about my own actions so that I can make amends for mistakes and misdeeds. Through this commitment I do my best to practice the Alcoholics Anonymous teaching to "put down the microscope and pick up the mirror." With the help of my spiritual inventories (see the Fourth Commitment, Chapter Six) I tell myself the truth about my mistakes and misdeeds with an eye to making amends. Amends help me to leave the past in the past and take a step towards restoring wholeness to the relationships I have damaged.

T'SHUVAH CAME FIRST (BEFORE THE CHICKEN AND THE EGG)

An obligation to make amends is woven deeply into the spiritual fabric of Judaism. The tradition teaches me that God put *t'shuvah* (amends) into the universe before putting human beings into the world. The reason is that God knew from the get-go that people would be imperfect, would make mistakes, and therefore would need a way to restore our souls and our relationships to wholeness. The *Kol Nidre* prayer, chanted during annual *Yom Kippur* services, reinforces the tradition of *t'shuvah*. The *Kol Nidre* prayer relieves people of the guilt and shame of past failures to carry out promises to act righteously. To make an amends is to take an action that carries out the *Kol Nidre* prayer. Through the amends process we are no longer weighed down by guilt and shame so that we have a better chance of acting more righteously in the future.

Steps Eight and Nine of the Alcoholics Anonymous Twelve Step program provide details that flesh out the amends process. Step Eight seeks to assure thorough amends by instructing members of the Twelve Step community to compile a list of all persons they have harmed and be willing to make amends to them all. Step Nine personalizes the amends process, calling for amends to be made to people directly wherever possible—"except when to do so would injure them or others."

Together, the spiritual traditions of Judaism and Alcoholics Anonymous teach me that making amends is one of the most crucial righteous actions I can take. I am human: I have made and I will continue to make mistakes. But the obligation to make amends means that I no longer have to fear, hide from or lie about my mistakes, or live in shame because of them. Amends offer me a pathway back to my soul, to the people I have wronged and to my community.

ECHOES

Making amends does not allow us to pretend that the past never happened. Amends cannot make the past disappear, any more than erasers (remember them?) can completely remove pencil marks from paper or delete buttons can remove electronic entries from computers' memories. Echoes of our past mistakes may remain forever in our consciences and in the consciousness of the people our actions have hurt or harmed. Lives taken away can never be restored, psychological wounds may never fully heal, and dignity stolen away may never be fully recaptured.

But making amends helps us to diminish the influence of our past mistakes on our future actions. When we make amends *our relationships do not have to be defined by our past mistakes.* If we cannot erase the past, amends make it possible for us to leave it behind so that we can begin to restore wholeness to our souls and to rebuild relationships with the people we have harmed.

REDEMPTION

Jewish tradition teaches me that people who are willing to move from the darkness into the light by making amends occupy a special place of redemption. The Hebrew word *t'shuvah* means "repentance," or more precisely, "turning from one's previous ways." The tradition celebrates the spiritual power of repentance and redemption through its teaching, "In the place where a repentant person stands, even the wholly righteous are not permitted to stand." At first glance, this teaching seems to elevate people who have behaved badly and repented over people who have always lived decently and are in no need of spiritual repentance. And in fact this teaching used to drive my brother Neal crazy! He was an esteemed rabbi and a respected figure in his community, he had always lived decently, and he had never been arrested or imprisoned. But once I turned my life around and became a "rehab rabbi," I was the brother who received publicity while Neal labored in relative obscurity. When Neal muttered about the unfairness of life (with his tongue partly in his cheek of course, because he is truly as proud of me as I am of him), all I could say was, "You're right Neal, life just isn't fair. The only fair I know about has a Ferris wheel."

Kidding with Neal aside, in my understanding the Jewish tradition does not establish a hierarchy of righteousness. When the tradition says that not even the most righteous person can stand where a repentant person stands, I understand it to mean that *all people are in need of repentance.* We are all imperfect, we all make mistakes, and we all need a pathway back to wholeness. That pathway is paved with amends.

MY AMENDS PROCESS

When I recognize the need to make amends, whenever possible I try to follow this "Three Steps" format:

- I apologize directly to the person I have wronged or harmed. (I try to do this personally, but I sometimes make "e-apologies.")
- I communicate my plan to do better in the future.
- I offer appropriate restitution.

STEP ONE: APOLOGY

Saying "I'm sorry" or "Oops I made a mistake" to the people we've harmed is not a complete amends, but it's a good start. An apology is a crucial first step because it demonstrates that we recognize the negative consequences of our actions and are not hiding from them.

STEP TWO: A PLAN TO DO BETTER

Step Two consists of verbalizing and then following through with a plan to do better from now on. Saying "sorry" and then returning to our old ways is not making amends! Even a brief and casual statement of a plan is likely to provide assurance that an amends is sincere and that we are willing to act righteously by following up our good words with good deeds.

By way of example, I offered amends recently to a Beit T'Shuvah resident after I had criticized the resident in front of his friends instead of privately. My amends statement, which I offered when the two of us were alone, went essentially like this:

> I'm sorry that I criticized you a couple of days ago in front of your friends. That was wrong of me. You and I have talked about your disrespectful attitude towards other residents before, and when I saw you behaving disrespectfully again I reacted too hastily in the heat of the moment. Even though I was bothered by your behavior, I should have arranged to talk to you about it when we were alone. I trust that you can do better. But if I need to talk to you about your behavior again, assuming there's no emergency I will wait to speak to you until we can get together in a private setting where you can feel comfortable responding to me.

My experience at making amends teaches me to avoid including explanations for mistakes in my plans to do better. For example, if I am making amends for unjust anger, I might be inclined to say something like, "The reason that I got so angry with you was that I had just come from an awful meeting with another resident." I have found however that explanations like this tend to be counter-productive. People tend to hear explanations as justifications, and think that if a similar scenario were to arise in the future I would quite probably commit a similar misdeed. As a result I generally avoid trying to explain away mistakes when I offer plans for doing better.

STEP THREE: OFFER RESTITUTION

By offering appropriate restitution, I do the best I can to restore what was lost to the people I have wronged through my mistake or misdeed. Lest a plan for restitution be doomed to fail at the outset, a plan must be realistic and reasonable from the perspective of the person who offers restitution. For example, assume that a resident had stolen $10,000 and lost it gambling before arriving at Beit T'Shuvah for treatment. The resident should not offer to make restitution by paying back the entire sum in a month if it is beyond the resident's capacity to do that. Instead, the resident might offer a more reasonable restitution plan based on periodic payments.

It may happen that what seems initially to be a reasonable restitution plan becomes unworkable. If so, our righteous obligation is to contact the person to whom we are making amends and change the terms of restitution. We might prefer to hide, but the best way for us to avoid the guilt and shame of being unable to live up to our promises is to face them and discuss them openly and honestly.

The appropriate measure of restitution is apparent when a misdeed results in the loss of money or specific items of property. But how do we make amends for the dignity that we stole or the trust that we betrayed? The only way that I know of to restore dignity and trust to a relationship is to emphasize our plan to do so and then to uphold that plan in our actions.

The most difficult restitution task of my life was restoring to my daughter Heather the trust that I stole from her by serving two terms in prison. She was three years old when I first went to prison. During that first term, her mom Linda (to whom I was then married) brought Heather to visit me almost every weekend. When I was released I promised Heather that I would never go back to prison. I was not able to keep that promise. Not long after I started serving my second term I got a letter from Heather, who was now seven years old. The letter said in part,

Daddy, I hate you. When you're in jail I'm in jail, and I didn't do anything to go to jail for. I hate you for that. It's not fair.

That letter broke my heart, but it helped change my life. I called Heather as soon as I could. I told her how very sorry I was and that what she had said in the letter was right. I told her how much studying and reading I had been doing. I swore to her that I had changed, that I loved her and that I would never go away again.

I knew that Heather had no reason to believe me. The only way that I could restore her trust in me was to demonstrate through my actions that I was no longer the man who kept disappearing from her life. I kept her letter in my wallet always, and I looked at it almost every day to remind myself of the damage I had done and my obligation to do everything in my power to restore Heather's trust in me. I couldn't do it all at once; Heather lived with her mom after we were divorced. But one day at a time I worked to make restitution. I showed up for her, and she for me through regular phone calls and get-togethers that helped me get through rabbinical school. We were even having fun! I have kept my promise never to leave her again—physically, emotionally or spiritually. For today we enjoy a trusting and loving relationship. We confide in each other, and we don't run away from our problems. We do our best to be a mirror of righteousness for each other. I seek to continue to make restitution to Heather every day of my life.

IF AT FIRST YOU DON'T SUCCEED...

We may offer amends to people who feel so victimized by our mistakes that even if they accept monetary restitution, they refuse to accept an apology, and they refuse to try to rebuild a relationship.

As the Serenity Prayer reminds us, we have no control over other people's actions. We cannot force people to accept our offers of amends if they choose not to do so. The Jewish tradition recognizes that some mistakes may be beyond the power of an amends to repair and actually offers a "solution" to this situation. The tradition teaches me to attempt to make amends three times. If the three attempts are unsuccessful—meaning that a person we hurt does not want to work towards repairing the relationship and moving forward together—we make *substituted amends*. We have then done all we can to restore the relationship to wholeness and we are then released from the guilt and shame of a misdeed.

Why does the tradition advise us to attempt to make amends even a second time? As I understand it, one attempt at making amends does not suffice because a wound may be too raw and a person too upset to genuinely hear and be in a position to accept a first offer of amends. When we attempt to make amends to the same person a second time, the tradition suggests that we bring along a friend or mentor who can vouch for our determination to repair the past and to do better going forward. If even the second attempt at amends is unsuccessful, the tradition teaches us to try a third time. (Perhaps this tradition is the origin of the phrase, "If at first you don't succeed, try and try again?") On the third attempt at making amends, the tradition suggests that we try to convince a wronged person to accept an offer of amends by bringing along a group of people to vouch for our sincerity. I cannot wholeheartedly endorse this aspect of the tradition. The presence of a group of people may seem more of a threat than a reassurance that an offer of amends is sincere! Then again, the tradition's suggested amends process arose a few centuries before the advent of electronic mail. Perhaps e-assurances of sincerity are a better way to adhere to this aspect of the tradition than showing up with a posse at our back!

It may be that even our third attempt at amends is unsuccessful. Or perhaps we cannot make amends directly to a person we have wronged because we are not aware of their identity. Our obligation then according to my understanding of the tradition is to make *substituted amends*. The need for substituted amends reflects the importance of the amends process to the spiritual growth of the makers of amends and not just to the recipients.

For example, I will never be able to apologize and make restitution to the actual victims who suffered because of the scams I perpetrated that landed me in prison twice. I do not even know who they are. But for the sake of my own spiritual growth. I act righteously by making substituted amends. Each year I donate a portion of my income to charitable groups that aid crime victims.

WHEN THE SHOE IS ON THE OTHER FOOT

Accepting other people's offers of amends to us is one way to diminish resentment and practice forgiveness (in accordance with my Second Commitment; see Chapter Four). When we build walls by refusing to accept genuine amends, we victimize ourselves by losing relationships that we might have been able to repair and strengthen going forward.

A TORAH DRASH

Everything Matters

The *parsha Naso* translates to "count/census." At first blush it was strange to me for the Torah to devote so many chapters to detailed counts and censuses. But as I reflect, I realize that the Torah is telling us that everything we do matters. This is actually a scary concept. I don't want everything to count! When I make mistakes I want mulligans and do-overs. I want to be able to erase, like I can when I do crossword puzzles in pencil. But we can't erase our actions; we can't pretend that the harms that we caused didn't happen. Though we can make amends, we can't deny that the negativity we created doesn't exist. What we accomplish through amends is to allow negativity to stay in the past rather than to permeate present and future moments. How long the negativity stays in the present depends on how long it takes us to make amends, and how long it takes for other people to accept them.

This can be hard. I realize how often I have carried old hurts and wounds that I caused and that were done to me. *Naso* tells me how much each of us and each of our actions matters. This portion tells me that I can no longer carry around the negativities of the past. I have to make amends for my mistakes and accept amends from other people. I also have to let go of old hurts and wounds even when the people who caused them do not make amends. Because I matter to myself, I cannot depend on the actions of others for my spiritual health. I need other people, and I need my communities. But I don't need to depend on others to release me from negativity so that I can live with joy and the knowledge that I matter.

SHARES FROM THE SHUV: MAKING AMENDS

A Shallow Apology
A Friend

I am in my mid-thirties; my addiction to drugs began when I started using at age eleven. My attempts at recovery have always failed. When I used,

I supported my drug habit by lying to family members and friends about why I needed money, and sometimes by stealing money from their purses and wallets and forging their signatures on checks.

Before I entered Beit T'Shuvah for what I will do my best to make my last stint in rehab, I told many of the people I had lied to and stolen from that I was sorry. I was sincere, and I got angry when they wouldn't believe me. They just kept telling me that they didn't trust me and wanted nothing to do with me. I think their rejection of me was one of the reasons that I went out again, went to jail, and ultimately became a resident of Beit T'Shuvah.

Beit T'Shuvah's counselors have helped me to understand why my victims did not believe my apologies. I hadn't been willing to talk to anyone about my lies and thefts, nor did my saying "sorry" give them any reason to believe that I would change my behavior from then on. My promises were what Mary Poppins called "pie crust promises"—easily made, easily broken. I know that at the end of the day, I can only regain people's trust through my actions. But I am committed to using my time at Beit T'Shuvah to understand the reasons for my mistakes and to figure out a plan to live decently when I move out, and then to communicate my plan to my victims when I apologize to them.

Starting Over
Jeff K.

My little sister Suzanne found me sleeping in the street, the morning after I had burgled a friend's mother's house and stolen food and items that I could sell to buy meth. I had been addicted to drugs virtually my entire life, and I was also battling bi-polar disorder. Suzanne and my older sister Jackie convinced me to seek help from Beit T'Shuvah. Rabbi Mark met with me during Rosh Hashanah prayers and by the evening I was cleaning the kitchen as the Shuv's newest resident.

Before that night I had made and lost millions of dollars as a stock broker and a producer of porn films. I lied to my business partners, lived apart from my wife after stealing from her inheritance, and did not speak to my father during the six months preceding his death. I also lost custody of my children; Jackie took them in as her own.

I was a terrible resident, and the Shuv did the right thing by throwing my ungrateful ass out after four months. That's when I finally started to pay attention. I lived with a friend but spent more time at the Shuv than when I was a resident. I found work as a salesman, made amends to my wife, and told Jackie and her family how grateful I was to them all for caring for my children. I have paid back thousands of dollars that I stole. Sadly, two people died before I could make amends to them. In one case I made amends to his wife; the other man's wife refused to see me. When I first moved into my own place so that I could re-unite with my wife and kids, I borrowed $7000 from the parents of a friend from Beit T'Shuvah. I sent them periodic money orders in small amounts for seven years, and repaid every penny of the loan.

Eight years into my recovery, my wife and I are closer than ever. My older son is in college and studying for the LSAT, and my younger son remembers little of the time we were apart. Jackie and I are very close and my career is going well, especially considering that I had to start over at age forty-six.

But every day is a challenge. Doing the next right things sounds simple, but often it is not. My sister Suzanne passed away and I have recently been battling cancer. And I still owe money to the Internal Revenue Service. But the lessons that I learned at the Shuv help me every day. I have many regrets in my life, but I am forever grateful that I let Jackie talk me into meeting with a loud, strong-willed and brilliant Rabbi Mark on Rosh Hashanah.

Payback Time
A Friend

I entered Beit T'Shuvah after my gambling addiction had destroyed my life. As a financial advisor, I essentially emptied out the bank account of any relative who was willing to believe my lies about my inside knowledge of "can't miss" companies. I was more than happy to support my lavish lifestyle by taking advantage of their desire to make easy money. I destroyed my family members' love and trust in my useless search for the big score that would allow me to pay off my gambling debts and return what I had stolen. Worst of all, I lost my wife and my children. I did time in federal prison, and four years later was paroled to Beit T'Shuvah. During those four years I apologized to each of the relatives I had victimized and told them that I would do my best to pay back what I had stolen once I was released.

When I moved out of Beit T'Shuvah I took a series of sales jobs. Though my earnings were modest, I followed through on my plan by committing to a schedule of payments with each of my victims. I promised to do the best I could to restore what I had stolen, and I also promised not to hide if I couldn't make a payment. I will probably never be able to repay everything I stole, but by living up to the plan to which I committed, I have begun to rebuild the sense of trust that I nearly destroyed. What amazes me the most is that my wife and children have accepted me back into their lives. We live modestly, but we have what we want.

Nursing Home Service
A Friend

I entered Beit T'Shuvah to seek recovery for my addiction to methamphetamines at a time when an elderly aunt I had always felt close to had developed dementia and had been moved to a nursing home. I was always meaning to visit her in the nursing home but I was arrested before I ever got there. Unfortunately my aunt died while I was in Beit T'Shuvah, before I had a chance to visit her. I felt awful and cried for the better part of a week because I had let drugs destroy my relationship with a beautiful soul who deserved much better from me. Since I couldn't make amends to my aunt, I committed to myself to give service as a volunteer in nursing homes, and spend time with residents who had no visitors.

Now that I am in a sober living house, I have followed through on this commitment. I also re-discovered my love of singing, and sometimes I get to sing for nursing home residents at events like Christmas parties. My substituted amends to the aunt who I let down continues to be a big part of my spiritual growth and commitment to stay sober and live better.

Lies My Parents Told Me
Jenny S.

I grew up thinking that my brother and I were twins and the natural children of our parents. Just before my twelfth birthday, I found out that each of us was adopted from a different family, and that my brother and I were born on different days. When I found out that my parents had lied to me my entire life about the circumstances and the date of my birth, I began lying to myself about myself. I told myself that I had no identity and that I did not matter—certainly not enough to be told the basic truth of my existence. I used these lies as an excuse to escape my distorted world. I began smoking marijuana at twelve, drinking alcohol at fifteen, and by the time I was thirty, all the years of alcohol abuse had taken its toll on my health. My liver began to fail—I was in constant pain and in a perpetual state of panic. One night I made a trip to the emergency room, and the doctor there told me I would likely die within six months if I didn't stop drinking. I detoxed two days later and checked into treatment seven days after that.

During my time as a resident of Beit T'Shuvah, I learned that my past does not have to dictate my present or my future. I realized that no matter what lies I believed as a child, I no longer have to believe them. I've learned to accept responsibility for my actions, and my actions alone. I know the truth of who I am and who I can grow to become. These truths transcend any lie my parents ever told me. Now that I am willing to look at myself honestly—to see me for me—I will not be defined by others' actions. Today, I live a life full of purpose and endless possibilities. There is nothing I can't do or be, as long as I remain truthful to myself about myself.

Beating Myself Up
A Friend

I am an addict and a convicted drug dealer. I caught a break when a judge who probably should have known better decided to give me one last chance to avoid going to prison by allowing me to serve my sentence in Beit T'Shuvah.

I arrived at Beit T'Shuvah knowing enough about its recovery program to know that I was supposed to be honest about who I was and what I had done. So I told my counselors honestly that I was a liar, a cheat and a thief. I told them that I had stolen from my family, from my suppliers and from the users who were my customers. I also was honest when I told them that I was a screw up who was too broken to contribute anything positive to the world.

What Beit T'Shuvah helped me to understand was that what I thought of as my willingness to be honest about myself was nothing more than a dishonest "pity party." Telling myself that I was worthless junk was a way for me to avoid doing the work by which I could change and become a decent person. This revelation blew me away. I was such an experienced liar that I lied to myself about telling the truth! I started to understand that no matter how badly I had lived before coming to Beit T'Shuvah, if I could be honest with myself about who I was and what I had done wrong I had a better chance to live decently from now on.

I am still in early recovery. I am not perfect, and I make mistakes even as a Beit T'Shuvah resident. But I am getting used to acknowledging instead of hiding from my mistakes and making amends for them. I believe that I am capable of living decently. While I can never erase the mistakes of my past, I can earn back trust by doing my best to live decently a day at a time.

CHAPTER TWELVE

TENTH COMMITMENT

I will not covet my neighbor's life; I will be grateful for my own life and for life itself.

THE TENTH COMMANDMENT instructs us not to covet the property of others. The commandment enumerates items of property that we are not to covet, such as a house and an ox. Some versions of the commandment deplorably include a wife among the examples. However, as I understand the commandment its instruction not to covet extends beyond tangible items of property. We also disobey the commandment when we lust after other people's lives and lifestyles.

My corollary tenth spiritual commitment is to be grateful for my own life and appreciative of life itself. Even as I try to be a grain of sand better tomorrow, I enjoy a richer and more meaningful life when my actions demonstrate my gratitude for who I am and what I have today.

OUR GREATEST VIRTUE

Rabbi Abraham Joshua Heschel taught that indifference to life is our biggest sin. If indifference is the greatest sin, then gratitude for life is the greatest virtue. My life is richer and more meaningful when my actions reflect my gratitude not merely for my life but for life itself. Abraham Lincoln famously said, "Folks are usually about as happy as they make up their minds to be." My corollary to President Lincoln's wisdom is, "Folks are usually about as grateful as they make up their minds to be." Disappointment and loss are inevitable features of life. Nevertheless I have much to be grateful for even during times of grief and sorrow.

I am grateful that at this moment I am alive.

I am grateful for the creativity and efforts of the people of previous generations that contributes so much to the life that I enjoy today. They were imperfect, and their eras were no less filled with injustice and violence than is mine. Nevertheless I can live the way I do now only because of their good works. I cannot thank them personally, but I can express my appreciation to them by acting righteously and sharing my blessings with others so that I can help pay forward to future generations the advantages that I am privileged to enjoy today.

I am grateful to live in obligation to a higher power of my understanding that provides me with an impulse to act righteously and the free will to take the next right action by wrestling with my conflicting desires to be selfish and selfless.

I am grateful that I have a program that provides me with tools for diminishing resentments by practicing forgiveness.

I am grateful for my spiritual partners and for the communities that support me, because they help me to stay right-sized and they remind me to practice my principles in all circumstances.

I am grateful that when I make a mistake, I have a spiritual program that teaches me to be transparent and honest so that I can when appropriate make amends and seek to restore broken relationships to wholeness.

I am grateful for my unique talents and passions that enable me to act with daily purpose.

I am grateful that each day and indeed each moment brings an opportunity for a new beginning, so that if I have missed the mark today I have the opportunity to do a grain of sand better tomorrow.

And I am grateful for the spiritual gift of hope, a gift that sustains my faith that all people will become willing to act a gain of sand more righteously so that a day at a time, the world becomes a more just, compassionate and peaceful place for all of its inhabitants.

GRATITUDE IS AN ACTION

Throughout this book I have stressed that the ten commitments focus on actions rather than on statements, intentions, beliefs or emotions. So it is with gratitude. *Gratitude is an action.* Acts reflecting gratitude for our blessings are righteous, and through those actions we enjoy richer and more meaningful lives. Below are tools that help me take actions that demonstrate my gratitude for life.

MORNING BLESSINGS

In accord with Jewish tradition, I act with gratitude through a daily recital of morning blessings. Numerous interpretations of this tradition exist. But the morning blessings tradition of my understanding—that is, the version of the tradition that is most meaningful for me—is to recite favorite morning blessings silently to myself before I get out of bed. These blessings include my gratitude for having lived to see another sunrise, for my soul, and for the gift of free will that allows me to pursue actions that reflect my conflicting desires to act selfishly and selflessly in proper measure. While I may sometimes recite additional blessings, what is most important to me is to start each day by reminding myself that whatever my troubles, I have much to be grateful for.

SPEAKING GRATITUDE

Putting gratitude into words keeps gratefulness present in my life and stimulates my daily pursuit of the next right action. Gratitude lists are one tool for speaking gratitude. Thinking through what I am grateful for in the moment helps me to act from gratitude and helps me to ward off my tendency to wallow in self-pity.

Another way to speak gratitude is to communicate to others our gratitude for righteous actions. All too often we comment on another person's behavior only when we find fault with it. Verbal expressions of gratitude for everyday decency provides recognition and stimulates both the givers and the recipients of gratitude to continue to act decently. Even a simple statement along the lines of, "I appreciate your taking care of that" is a reminder that we are all kin, that we don't do anything alone, and that we appreciate opportunities to be of service to others and to accept help from others.

Gratitude loves company. As it is with many meetings of Alcoholics Anonymous and other Twelve Step groups, gratitude sessions are a regular part of Friday night services at Beit T'Shuvah. Residents and congregants have an opportunity to speak their gratitude as a part of a community. For example, family members or friends of residents who are celebrating sober birthdays may express gratitude for a resident's return to health and commitment to living well. Residents may express gratitude for a kind word or deed of friendship that provided a much-needed lift. And each week I express my gratitude for the previous week's events that provide me with a life that I could never have imagined when I was an addict in the depths of my disease. I also give gratitude for the people who helped me to make it safely and successfully through the previous week. For instance, I often thank my mentor Rabbi Ed Feinstein for his willingness to discuss our different understandings of a weekly Torah portion, and I may thank employees and congregants for their willingness to help people to live well. My last gratitude is always for my wife Harriet, for the actions through which she continues to demonstrate her love for me despite my faults, and for her efforts in keeping alive the soul of Beit T'Shuvah and refusing to leave anyone behind.

TZEDAKAH

The Jewish tradition of *tzedakah* echoes the giving practices of many other religious and spiritual traditions. *Tzedakah* often consists of contributing money to people or to the institutions that help to feed and clothe them. But in the Jewish tradition, *tzedakah is not charity*. We may *choose* to give to charity. But *tzedakah* is not a matter of choice; it is a spiritual obligation of righteous people. Through *tzedakah* we demonstrate gratitude that we *get to* act righteously by sharing what we have with others. The obligation to give *tzedakah* means that *everyone* can demonstrate righteousness because the obligation extends to the neediest people among us, including those who are themselves recipients of *tzedakah*. Through the practice of *tzedakah*, all people know that they matter, all people have a seat at the table and all people have a path to righteousness.

While practicing *tzedakah* produces physical benefits for recipients, *tzedakah* produces *spiritual* benefits for givers. *Tzedakah* strengthens our souls and our commitment to act righteously by reminding us that we are all holy souls, that we are all kin, and that we all have an obligation to do what we can to help each other live decently. *Tzedakah* helps us lay down bridges rather than erect walls, because giving *tzedakah* helps us to see parts of ourselves in others.

Some years ago, in a presentation to graduate business students at UCLA, community philanthropist Eli Broad spoke of his gratitude for the opportunity to share his wealth with the public. As much as he had enjoyed his life in business, nothing brought him greater satisfaction and enriched his soul more than using his wealth to help people live decently and with joy. Of course I have nowhere near the wealth of Eli Broad. But that is exactly the point. I too experience a spiritual connection to humanity through the practice of *tzedakah,* and that connection is available to all of us, regardless of our financial status.

The practice of *tzedakah* is so central to the Jewish concept of living decently that the twelfth century Jewish sage Maimonides described eight distinct levels of *tzedakah.* You have probably heard of the aphorism that "If you give a person a fish, the person can eat for a day. But if you teach a person to fish, the person can eat for a lifetime." Maimonides' eight levels of *tzedakah* are a much older (and less fishy) statement of this principle. The lowest level of *tzedakah* is to donate money grudgingly to those who are in need; the highest form of *tzedakah* is to teach people to be productive, so they can support themselves. At Beit T'Shuvah we do our best to embody Maimonides' eighth level of *tzedakah.* Our commitment is to help people lead useful and productive lives of recovery, not simply to achieve sobriety. To that end Beit T'Shuvah pursues opportunities to offer residents externships, in-house job experience, and career and educational services.

MITZVOT (GOOD DEEDS)

We can also express our gratitude for life by performing *mitzvot,* "good deeds." Each good deed injects us with positive energy that stimulates our soul's impulse to act righteously.

The spiritual benefits of good deeds are embedded in the traditions of Alcoholics Anonymous and Judaism. A.A. calls on its members to be of service to other addicts. Good deeds through which members of A.A. do service include serving as a sponsor, taking people to meetings, and carrying the message of A.A. to others (the twelfth step).

In Judaism, the Bar and Bat Mitzvah traditions ("Bar" for boys, "Bat" for girls) exemplify the concept of reflecting gratitude for life through performing good deeds. People often mistakenly use these terms as verbs, such as by saying, "My best friend's daughter was bat mitzvahed last week." The truth is that these terms are nouns, not verbs. In other words, a child (and in modern times many adults too) who completes the training and goes through the proper ceremony becomes a bar (or bat) mitzvah. By *becoming* a bar or bat mitzvah a person takes on an obligation to carry out good deeds and act righteously.

Whatever our talents, interests and uniqueness of purpose, we have so many opportunities to carry out good deeds! Not so long ago a popular phrase urged people to perform "random acts of kindness." Random acts of kindness can be anonymous, such as when we pay a bridge toll for the driver of the car behind us, pass up an empty parking space so another person can use it, and smile at a passerby.

Performing good deeds often requires little time or effort. For example, if I happen to know the name of store clerk who has helped me, or I see the clerk's name on a badge, I can thank the clerk by name. Even this seemingly insignificant gesture communicates, "I see you as an individual, not just an employee, and I appreciate you." I may contact a former classmate with whom I have lost touch just to check in, and not because I need a favor or information. I may send a note of appreciation to a resident or a congregant for a thoughtful share during Friday night Sabbath services, for a small kindness or for any other action that brings a little bit more light into the world.

Not long ago, I attended a presentation by one of the most well-known philosophers in the country. He provided fascinating speculations about the meaning of the ways in which Michelangelo's treasured Sistine Chapel paintings depicting the story of Adam and Eve diverge from the story of Adam and Eve in *Genesis,* the first book in the Bible. After the presentation, I sent him a short email that simply thanked him for a stimulating talk. This eminent and often-honored philosopher responded, "I am so pleased you cared for what I said. It means a great deal to me…I shall not forget that." The term *mitzvot* may suggest performance of services on behalf of needy people. But even for those who have achieved much, a small and simple act of *mitzva* can produce great joy.

Volunteer work allows us to act on a talent or interest that we might not otherwise use in daily life. For instance, those among us who have an ability to sing but who are not professional singers may entertain senior residents of an assisted living facility. Others of us might be able to paint a room or perform simple repairs for people who cannot afford to hire a professional. Our volunteer work may be regular and ongoing, or sporadic and varied. Whatever we choose to do, and however we choose to do it, we implicitly reflect gratitude for life and stimulate our impulse to live a richer and more meaningful life when we perform good deeds.

DISAPPOINTMENT, GRIEF AND GRATITUDE

None of us lives a fairytale life of "happily ever after." We all experience losses and disappointments that produce sadness and grief. We cannot eliminate or paper over these feelings by reminding ourselves of our blessings. Nor should we want to, because unhappy feelings are part of our humanity. But when we are ready—not to forget, but to move forward—reflecting gratitude for life through our actions can limit the power of sadness and grief to control our actions.

When I was a teenager I experienced intense grief when the father I adored suffered a sudden heart attack and died. I cannot blame that event for my descent into addiction and crime. But while the pain of my father's loss has never left me, my obligation is to make sure that the pain does not prevent me from acting righteously and living a rich and meaningful life. Gratitude for my life and for our shared lives helps me to fulfill this obligation. I often speak my gratitude for my father's wisdom, kindness and commitment to justice for all people. And I reflect my gratitude to him in my actions by trying in my own life to further the purposes and principles he exemplified but can no longer pursue.

Gratitude can also help us to sustain recovery from the maladies of our soul. Beit T'Shuvah has for many years hosted a weekly Alcoholics Anonymous meeting that we call *L'Chaim*, "To Life," The meeting is open to all in the recovery community who want to attend. A few years ago the lead speaker at one *L'Chaim* meeting was an African-American woman in her sixties. She told the group that she had spent the bulk of her life in prison. She had served five terms for crimes she committed to sustain her addiction to heroin, and every family member and friend in her life had given up on her. Yet the focus of her share that night was gratitude and hope. Each time she was released on parole, she left prison with the hope that she could live with decency and purpose. Yet not until she was about sixty years old had she replaced intentions with actions. She took classes in prison and when she was released went to work for a social service agency. She told the meeting about the programs she runs in L.A. and the conferences she participates in all across the country. She remembers to be grateful each day for the impulse to act righteously that she ignored for years but could never entirely squelch, an impulse that allowed her to change when she was willing to use her unique talents, experiences and interests to live with daily purpose. A day at a time, she continued to work to rebuild relationships with the family members and friends who long ago had given up on her.

A TORAH DRASH

Moses' Ethical Will

The *parsha Devarim* translates to "words/things" and records Moses' last words to his people Israel before his death. I think of this as Moses' Ethical Will to the people of Israel and the world. Moses knows at this point that he is going to die without achieving the "prize" of getting into the Promised Land. He is going to die without reaping the rewards of his labors over the previous forty years of wandering in the desert. As I read *Devarim* now, I had a profound awakening of realizing how much emphasis I put on winning and reaping the rewards of my labor. This Torah portion teaches me that the "rewards" and the "prize" consist of gratitude for each moment that we can be present and have the opportunity to do the best we can. When we are present in our lives we can be grateful for the beauty, joy and satisfaction that each moment can bring to us.

SHARES FROM THE SHUV: GRATITUDE

Time to Confess
Martin S.

Sins are often actions that harm others, acts that involve theft, violence, lying and cheating. There are also self-inflicted sins, such as in my case alcoholism. But the sin to which I want to confess here is my misuse of time. I have been indifferent to its value, and ungrateful for the gift of time that has been given to me. I have stolen time from myself, and I have been a slave to time.

I have heard Rabbi Ed Feinstein speak of the pagan notion that time exists as a Circle of Life. In this circle of sunrises and sunsets, every day is a repetition of the day before, nothing changes, and what was always will be. By contrast, the Jewish view of time is expressed in the opening words of the Torah, *Bereishit,* "In the Beginning." In the Jewish tradition, every day is a new beginning. Every day and indeed every moment is filled with the possibility of change, the possibility of the new and the different, the possibility of choice, the possibility of love and connection, the possibility of surprise, and the possibility of living in what Rabbi Abraham Joshua Heschel called "radical amazement of life." So I ask myself, "How do I escape the shackles of time?" "How do I find the timeless within the limits of time?" The answer for me is not simple because the march of time is inexorable. But if there is not an answer, at least there is a response. And my response is *t'shuvah,* to seek forgiveness from God and from myself for my indifference to the gift of time, which is after all the gift of life.

So I value the gift of time through gratitude for the precious things I have and have had in my life: my parents of blessed memory who loved me unconditionally; a loving family who always supported me; children who grew into independent and caring adults; a cherished grandson; the opportunity to work with people who inspire me with their dedication, passion, and compassion; my health and my sobriety; and the opportunity and privilege to give back to others in need. I am grateful for the time I have been given to honor and show respect for those who have given me so much.

Lying to Myself
Paul S.

When I first arrived at Beit T'Shuvah, I was filled with incredible shame—pitiful and incomprehensible demoralization. Who was this person that I had become? A stranger? A total loser? After three previous rehab programs and yet another relapse, I believed that I was simply a depraved, tortured spirit who, unlike Midas, turned everything I touched into garbage.

My story, at least the one I told myself, was that I was far more pathetic than my Beit T'Shuvah housemates. Not only did I have a family and successful career, but I was also an ordained rabbi with a considerable reputation as an author and educator. I lived and taught in the spiritual transformation business and I still wrecked my life!

After a few weeks of spiraling through the depths of agonizing humiliation, I began to wake up to a new possibility of life. I began to understand that I could not continue to divide my inner world from my outer one. Previously, I believed that if my external self—job, reputation, achievements, possessions—was in order then my internal self would also be in order. I thought I could manage a breach of personal integrity because I wasn't really "hurting anyone else." But after facing my Judaism, my community, my own self, and my God, I knew that if I wanted to live, I had to admit that alcohol only temporarily pacified my internal split, and that I had to honestly reckon with my pain.

Recovery is not easy and being a rabbi in recovery doesn't make it any easier. I lost just about everything for which I had worked so hard due to alcoholism. I also, however, gained a sense of freedom that I hadn't known before. Today I know gratitude. Getting sober was the beginning of a new life; it marked a new season for me to teach and preach again, not just by talking about spiritual transformation, but by living it one day at a time.

Letting Go of the Past
Lindsay P.

When I was a kid my family was divided and I bounced around from place to place. I felt like I was not good enough, and to hide those feelings of inadequacy I started using drugs and alcohol as a teenager. By the time I was in my early twenties I was hanging around with drug dealers. I knew what I was doing was wrong but I was desperate for a place to belong. I was in and out of jails, I was in an abusive relationship, and I gave birth to a child that was taken away from me.

I was released from jail with nothing to my name but ten months of sobriety and an overwhelming fear of the world. Close friends helped me find Beit T'Shuvah, which gave me a chance even though I was penniless. After a few months in "the house" I found a job as an office assistant, and it has helped me let go of who I was. I have a husband whom I met in the house, and we have a son. I have learned that I am good enough, and each day I strive to be better than I was the day before. I have been sober for nearly three years, and I am so grateful to have the life I had always been searching for.

The Music of My Soul
Rose H.

Ten years ago, I moved to L.A. to work in the entertainment industry. For the first few years, I was very fortunate to have opportunities to do what I loved. However, everything began to change as my drug addiction took over. My life became smaller and smaller, until I stopped caring about all the things that had meant so much to me: health, relationships, purpose and even my will to live.

I came into the house broken and lost, Beit T'Shuvah gave me a place to heal and recover my soul. I've run a marathon, pursued my lifelong passion for music and songwriting, and I am privileged to share my message of hope with others. Today I have a life beyond my wildest dreams, and I am eternally grateful for my life and for the kindness and compassion of the entire community.

CHAPTER THIRTEEN

APPENDIX

Rabbi Mark's Holiness Code

THE HOLINESS CODE is a common name for a lengthy series of laws in the section of the book of the Bible called Leviticus. This Appendix sets forth my personal holiness code. Since I act decently through continued willingness to question my actions, my personal holiness code consists of questions rather than laws. The questions below, based on the Ten Commitments, help me to act holy. Holiness is not a quality that is reserved for saints, the clergy or religious adherents. A spark of holiness is within each of us, but it is up to us to reflect this spark through our actions. Here are questions that I often ask myself in an effort to act a grain of sand more holy each day than I did the day before.

How adequately do my deeds live up to my commitments?

How am I carrying on the good works of my parents and other ancestors? Realizing that my forebears were no more perfect than I am, I cannot use their mistakes as an excuse to ignore what they did well.

How do I make time to appreciate what is good about my life, my communities and the world?

How do I enjoy my material possessions without regarding them as indispensable to my life?

How do I want what I have rather than needing to have what I want?

How well do I balance taking care of myself with my desire to share my time, values, experiences and material goods with others?

How well do I reflect my holiness and respect for others in my everyday encounters?

When is it more important for me to maintain a relationship than to insist that I am right?

How willing am I to seek out and listen to others?

When am I too headstrong or fearful of seeming weak to ask for help?

How successfully do I refuse to take unfair advantage of the vulnerability, ignorance or weakness of others?

How willing am I to demonstrate respect for the people I care about by being honest with them when their actions miss the mark?

How willing am I to see the parts of other people that I don't like in myself?

How well do I focus on becoming the best version of me that I can instead of comparing myself to other people?

How well do I show up and speak up for people who are powerless?

How well do I demonstrate to people who are ill in body, mind or spirit that they are holy souls who matter to me, whether or not I can do anything to restore them to good health?

How willing am I to be honest with people who have wronged me and to talk to them in a way that they can understand?

How willing am I to accept amends and to diminish resentment by practicing forgiveness?

How well do I separate myself from the guilt and shame of my past mistakes so that I am better able to approach each moment as an opportunity to do better?

How well do my actions reflect respect for my dignity and the dignity of others?

Printed in the United States
By Bookmasters